D1594186

Series/Number 07-142

PROBABILITY THEORY
A PRIMER

TAMÁS RUDAS
Eötvös Loránd University, Budapest
and
TÁRKI Social Research Centre

SAGE PUBLICATIONS
International Education and Professional Publisher
Thousand Oaks   London   New Delhi

For information:

Sage Publications, Inc.
2455 Teller Road
Thousand Oaks, California 91320
E-mail: order@sagepub.com

Sage Publications Ltd.
1 Oliver's Yard
55 City Road
London, EC1Y 1SP
United Kingdom

Sage Publications India Pvt. Ltd.
B-42, Panchsheel Enclave
Post Box 4109
New Delhi 110 017 India

Printed in the United States of America on acid-free paper.

Library of Congress Cataloging-in-Publication Data

Rudas, Tamás.
Probability theory : a primer / Tamás Rudas.
p. cm. — (Quantitative applications in the social sciences ; 142)
Includes bibliographical references.
ISBN 0-7619-2506-6 (pbk. : acid-free paper)
1. Probabilities. I. Title. II. Series: Sage university papers series. Quantitative applications in the social sciences ; no. 142.
QA273.R8815 2004
519.2—dc22

2004000163

04   05   06   07   08   09   10   9   8   7   6   5   4   3   2   1

Acquiring Editor:	Lisa Cuevas Shaw
Editorial Assistant:	Margo Crouppen
Project Editor:	Claudia A. Hoffman
Copy Editor:	Liann Lech
Typesetter:	C&M Digitals (P) Ltd.

CONTENTS

Contents

SERIES EDITOR'S INTRODUCTION

Probability theory forms the basis of statistical inference in social science research. We have no "iron laws," only probabilistic ones, because of the uncertainty inherent in the study of human behavior. For example, suppose there is a research study, where it is hard to say "for sure" that certain banks discriminate (or not) in awarding home loans to Hispanic applicants. Perhaps a higher turndown rate is due to chance, or to some other factor that has nothing to do with ethnicity. Statistical tests can rule out rival hypotheses and reject the argument that there is no difference between, for instance, Hispanic and White applicants. But they cannot show with 100% certainty that discrimination of this kind exists in the population at large. Nevertheless, for lawmakers and political activists, it may be enough for the results to suggest that unfair practices seem highly probable.

The monograph at hand is a beginner's guide to probability theory, covering the most often used distributions in the social sciences—the binomial, the normal, and the chi-square. Probability treats uncertainty, dealing with stochastic as opposed to deterministic models. The author's approach is frequentist, taking the view that a fixed value in the population is generating outcomes. An event has a probability, and that probability is uncovered through repeated trials over time. There is the probability of a particular coin tossing heads, or the contemporary political example of the probability of a president's reelection. Probabilities are never really known in advance, but instead are retrieved from relative frequencies observed over trials.

In Chapter 2, relative frequency properties are discussed, such as the following: A relative frequency must be between 0 and 1; the relative frequency of an opposite event is 1, the relative frequency of the event; the relative frequency of a certain event = 1; two events cannot occur at the same time. In Chapter 3, the concepts of independence, additivity, and density functions are explicated. Histograms, with their intervals, may approximate density functions. The density function of a normal distribution is represented by a very refined histogram, where the intervals are probabilities.

Chapter 4 discusses probability distributions and random variables. The most elementary probability distribution is the uniform distribution. In the discrete case, a random variable simply equals its different values and their probabilities. For example, the variable of Political Party Identification, with 33% of the surveyed voters saying they are Republican, 40% Democrat, and 27% Independent, makes a probability distribution with probabilities, vi

respectively, of .33, .40, and .27. The expected value of this random variable would be the average of these values. The normal distribution is continuous, and extremely important for social statistics. It is not a single distribution, but rather a family of probability distributions, all of which share the property of being bell-shaped. The standard normal distribution has an expected value equal to 0 and variance equal to 1. The probability of a standard normal variable deviating from 0 by a value greater than 2.00 is less than .05. This property is the basis of the significance test, where the null hypothesis of, say, $\beta = 0$, is rejected at the .05 level, suggesting with 95% certainty that the relationship exists in the population.

This little handbook could be read in any introductory social science data analysis course when the instructor wishes to supplement the usual textbook readings, which too often restrict themselves to examples from the play of dice, cards, or colored balls. Here, Professor Rudas employs, among others, the more useful example of consumer behavior and the purchase of different products from different companies.

—*Michael S. Lewis-Beck*
Series Editor

1. INTRODUCTION

Probabilities and probabilistic arguments are interwoven into every aspect of modern life, from quality control to weather forecasting, investment decisions, and gambling, and from election forecasting to designing power networks. Probability theory provides us with a framework for dealing with situations in the presence of uncertainty. The methods for obtaining estimates and reaching decisions in such situations are discussed in mathematical statistics. Uncertainty in the social sciences arises for several reasons. The most important among them is the fact that data are not typically collected from everyone in the population of interest. Instead, usually only a small fraction (the sample) is interviewed. One can never be completely sure whether those not interviewed would have given responses similar to those who actually responded. Fortunately, if the sample is appropriately selected, generalization of the findings from the sample to the population can be justified. Such random (or probability) sample selection methods are now used routinely in the social sciences and in many other fields of empirical investigation. The method of sample selection also has to be taken into account when choosing the methods of data analysis and in interpreting the results. There are other sources of uncertainty, including imprecise knowledge, the limitations of measurement procedures, and misleading or incomplete information. These uncertainties need to be taken into account both in data collection and analysis, and in more general conceptual thinking about the main research issues in the social sciences. Uncertainty is usually incorporated into our thinking by applying probabilistic arguments.

Probability theory, therefore, is the relevant frame of reference in both data collection and data analysis. The aim of this book is to give a nontechnical introduction to the main concepts of probability theory as it is applied in the social sciences.

Chapter 2 introduces the concept of probability by discussing two fundamentally different ways of thinking about observing reality: One can assume either that what is known or observed (essentially) implies the results, or that uncertainty still remains. Although there is general agreement that the latter approach is appropriate for scientific experiments and observational studies, and that probability theory provides us with the formalized rules for arriving at relevant conclusions when uncertainty is present, there are different ways of defining the concept of probability. These different approaches lead to practically the same notion of probability, and the one presented here yields the important properties of probability in the most intuitive way. The so-called *frequentist approach* says that probabilities are numbers that govern the outcomes of the observational procedure and can be detected by repeated observations. The results of the repeated observations are best summarized using relative frequencies of the outcomes or events. The properties of relative frequencies can be used to explore the properties of probability. In most applications, the number of outcomes or events associated with an experiment is finite, but, as it turns out, assuming infinitely many different outcomes can be a useful approximation in many practical situations, and this is also explained.

Chapter 3 discusses those properties of probability that are relevant in applying it to problems often occurring in the social sciences. Probabilities are assigned to the outcomes or events associated with a certain experiment or observational study. The most important property of probability is a kind of additivity applying to disjoint (nonoverlapping) events. The concept and importance of this additivity in the case of infinitely many outcomes is also outlined. All of these properties are derived from the relevant properties of relative frequencies.

In Chapter 4, probability distributions and random variables are introduced. These are efficient concepts for handling all possible outcomes and their probabilities at the same time, and for summarizing the description of the entire experiment or observational study in the presence of uncertainty. From a social scientist's point of view, the most important probability distributions are the binomial, the normal, and the chi-squared distributions, and these are discussed in turn. The binomial distribution and its generalization, the multinomial distribution, give straightforward descriptions of situations with a small number of different observations and can be discussed with relatively simple means. The normal distribution gives a good approximation in many practical situations when the number of different outcomes is large, and also in situations when the sample size is large. The chi-squared distribution is frequently applied in testing statistical hypotheses and is discussed here with reference to those applications.

Chapter 5 contains a brief summary of the material discussed in the book.

2. WHERE DO PROBABILITIES COME FROM?

Many of the data available in the social sciences come from surveys that employ random sampling (see Kalton, 1983). Random sampling has several variants, but in its simplest form, it implies that everybody in the population has the same chance of being selected into the sample, or that everyone in the population has the same selection probability. This chapter is devoted to the discussion of the concept of probability.

2.1 Deterministic and Stochastic Models

Every form of empirical scientific inquiry observes its subject under standardized circumstances. Standardization is important for comparison, interpretation, and conclusion. In the life sciences, observations are typically made under conditions determined by the researcher. For example, in order to assess the effect of smoking on mammals, laboratory rats are exposed to cigarette smoke, with the researcher determining the length of exposure and the actual content of the smoke. In order to be able to decide which components of the findings can be attributed to smoking, the researcher needs a so-called control group, that is, rats not exposed to cigarette smoke. The results are obtained from a comparison of the findings in the two groups. It is up to the researcher to determine which rat gets into the exposed group and which into the nonexposed group. Group membership is usually determined in such a way as to make the groups as similar as possible (except, of course, the difference with respect to smoking). Similarity is usually achieved by random assignment of rats to the two groups. Random assignment may not yield identical groups in an experiment, but over a series of experiments, it justifies the assumption of identical groups. In the social sciences, in most cases, the conditions of observation are not entirely determined by the researcher. For example, in order to assess the potential effect of smoking on medical expenditures, the researcher may want to compare the expenditures of two groups of people, one smoking and the other nonsmoking. It would be beneficial to have two groups identical in every aspect (except for smoking or not), because in this case, if a difference were found, it could be attributed to smoking. Unfortunately, it is impossible to have two identical groups of people, one smoking and one not. The researcher may try to make the two groups as similar as possible in every aspect (age, gender, socioeconomic status, etc.), yet the two groups will remain fundamentally different: One will consist of people who—for some reason—choose to smoke, and the other will consist of people who choose not to smoke. This difference cannot be eliminated: With rats, it is the researcher who decides who smokes and who does not; with people, it is the people themselves–and people making different choices cannot be assumed identical.

The first type of data collection (where the researcher has practically unlimited potential for intervention and can achieve virtually identical groups) is called an *experiment* (see Brown & Melamed, 1990; Levin, 1999). The second type of data collection (where the researcher has to cope with decisions made by the subjects themselves and cannot achieve identical groups) is called an *observational study* (see Rosenbaum, 1995). Experiments and observational studies need to be clearly distinguished. For example, experiments, if properly designed, are usually considered appropriate for reaching causal conclusions (if the rats in the smoking group die earlier than the rats in the nonsmoking group, it can be attributed to smoking), but observational studies usually are not appropriate for reaching causal conclusions. (If the smoking group happens to have higher medical expenses than the nonsmoking group, it cannot necessarily be attributed to smoking. It may, for example, be a consequence of a physiological peculiarity that makes the group members smoke and would lead to the same medical conditions and expenses even if these people did not smoke.) In spite of this fundamental difference, any form of making observations under standardized circumstances will be called an experiment in what follows. Standardization here means that the researcher has to determine how observations are made and what the possible *outcomes* are, in every relevant detail. For example, the researcher has to determine how to obtain the rats, how to distribute them between the two groups, how long one group is exposed to smoke, and so on, but also that the outcomes are the deaths or survivals of the particular rats after a certain period of time. Or, the researcher has to determine how smokers and nonsmokers are selected into the sample, what expenses count toward medical expenditures, how these expenses are recorded, and so on, but also that the outcomes are certain dollar figures for the average expenditures of both groups. Outcomes are exclusive; that is, after having finished the experiment, the researcher is able to decide which outcome occurred, and there is always one, and only one, outcome that occurred.

Certain combinations of outcomes may be more interesting than the outcomes themselves. For example, if rats A, B, and C are exposed to smoke and rats D, E, and F are not, one may be interested as to whether more rats in the exposed group die than in the nonexposed group. This is the case if only A dies, or only B, or only C, or if A and B die or B, C, and E die or A, B, C, D, and E die, and so on. Such combinations are called *events*. In the other example, an interesting event may be that during the study period, the average medical expenditure of the smoking group is higher than that of the nonsmoking group. Again, this event may occur in many different ways. For example, this event occurred if the average expenditure of the smoking group was $2,000 and that of the nonsmoking group $1,750 (which is an outcome), or if the values were $500 and $300, respectively (another outcome). Notice that the outcomes are also events.

Having defined the experiment (the conditions of observation, the possible outcomes, the relevant events), the researcher may take either one of two positions. One standpoint would assume that the conditions determine entirely which outcome will occur; the other would say that uncertainty still remains as to the actual outcome. In the first case, the researcher uses a *deterministic model,* and in the second case, a *stochastic model.* In a popular high school experiment, an object is dropped from a certain height (say, 10 feet), and the time it takes before it hits the floor is measured. The deterministic view of this experiment is that the height from which the object is dropped determines entirely the outcome (the time), and the experiment is appropriate for computing the acceleration of gravity. In another deterministic experiment, prior to this one, the experimenter may assume that the height and also the mass of the object dropped are both relevant; it can be determined that the latter quantity is not relevant by dropping objects of different weights (e.g., a larger and a smaller key) from the same height. Deterministic experiments are important tools of scientific research. In a deterministic experiment, the conditions are supposed to determine the outcome, but not in a way known to the experimenter before the experiment is actually performed.

The same experiment can also be given a stochastic interpretation. Unless one uses a very expensive instrument to measure the time it takes for the dropped object to hit the floor, the result will contain some error, and the magnitude of this may be quite substantial. Imprecise measurements are, in general, a very important source of uncertainty. The actual size of the measurement error is not known, although certain rules governing its typical size may be known. Another source of uncertainty is that air resistance may influence the results, and the experimenter may have no theory to describe this influence. However, for certain objects (like a key), this effect is known to be small. The lack of sufficiently precise theory is another general source of uncertainty. These are uncertainties concerning the result of the experiment. A further uncertainty is present in terms of deciding whether the results are true generally or there are certain limitations. The experiment may be performed with different objects of different masses and with different heights, but not with all possible objects and all possible heights. Or, if the measurements are precise enough, it may turn out that the altitude at which the experiment is performed is also relevant. In general, the issue of the generalization of the findings from the actual observations to objects that were not actually observed is another important source of uncertainty.

Certainty can rarely be complete or absolute. Deterministic models are approximations only, and they are useful in developing or confirming scientific theories. Scientific theories (and everyday knowledge, for that matter) can also be deterministic or stochastic (if a car is driven without coolant, the engine will be damaged—deterministic; or, there may be a rainbow after rain—stochastic). Very often, a scientific theory consists of both deterministic and stochastic components.

The usefulness of deterministic models and related theories, if they are available in a given situation, is clear. What are stochastic models and theories good for? The way in which stochastic models contribute to our understanding becomes apparent if different models with the same outcomes are compared. One can say that there may be a rainbow after rain because this is sometimes true and sometimes not. Here, the outcomes that one observes are the presence or lack of a rainbow. One can also say that there may be a rainbow after rain if the sun shines. This experiment has the same outcomes as the previous one, but the circumstances of observation are different. In the second case, sunshine is also assumed, and therefore, the experiments are different. If both experiments are repeated, say, 100 times, a rainbow will occur less often among repetitions of the first experiment (observing the sky after rain) than among the repetitions of the second experiment (observing the sky after rain if the sun shines). We refer to this fact by saying that the probability of a rainbow is lower in the first experiment than in the second one. Stochastic models can be helpful in discovering relevant information with respect to the outcomes (namely, that sunshine is necessary for a rainbow to occur).

It has to be kept in mind that, very often, the choice between a deterministic and a stochastic model is up to the researcher. The choice depends on the circumstances of the scientific inquiry (exploratory or confirmatory), and also on the level of certainty (or uncertainty) involved. When the outcome is fairly certain, a deterministic model may be appropriate, but if the outcome of the experiment is fairly uncertain, a stochastic model— incorporating uncertainty—may be more relevant. As knowledge accumulates regarding the topic of the experiment, the conditions of the experiment can be redefined, for example, by taking conditions necessary for a certain outcome—such as sunshine for a rainbow—into account. When the conditions imply the outcome—possibly after a long series of experiments with changing conditions—the model turns into a deterministic model.

2.2 Frequentist and Other Approaches

The concept of probability proposed at the end of the previous section is that probability is a property of an outcome (or, more generally, an event) associated with an experiment that influences the frequency of the occurrence of this outcome (or, more generally, the event). Larger probability means that the event occurs more frequently; smaller probability means that the event occurs less frequently. This definition of probability has a very important implication: It directly leads to a quantification of probability, that is, to the conclusion that probability is a quantity (a number) associated with the events of an experiment. Furthermore, the frequency with which an event occurs can be used to estimate the probability of that event, and general properties of probability are easily derived from the properties of (relative) frequencies.

Our approach to probability is called *frequentist* because it derives the concept of probability from the concept of frequency. More specifically, the probability is related to the *relative frequency*. If an experiment is repeated a certain number of times, the number of those repetitions when a specified event occurred is the frequency of that event. The relative frequency is obtained by dividing the frequency by the number of times the experiment was repeated.

For example, assume one is interested in the reelection of U.S. presidents. The experiment of interest is to observe the U.S. presidential elections, but only those when the incumbent has an opportunity to be reelected, that is, only elections after a president's first term. The outcomes that one observes are whether or not the president in office was reelected. This experiment is repeated for the past 20 years, in 1984 (after the first term of Reagan), in 1992 (after the first term of Bush), and in 1996 (after the first term of Clinton). Therefore, the experiment is repeated three times. The frequency of reelection is two (Reagan and Clinton were reelected after their respective first terms), and the frequency of no reelection is one (only Bush was not reelected). The relative frequency of reelection is 2/3, and the relative frequency of no reelection is 1/3. The properties of relative frequencies will be studied further in the next section.

To clarify the relationship between probabilities and relative frequencies, assume an experiment is repeated in several long sequences. For every sequence, the relative frequency of an event is calculated. That is, one obtains a number for every sequence (for a particular event). Now, let us focus our attention on situations when these figures are not very different. This situation is called *stability of the relative frequencies*. More precisely, consider experiments and events such that the relative frequencies can be made arbitrarily close to each other by choosing long-enough sequences. In other words, by choosing long-enough sequences, the relative frequencies get arbitrarily close to a common value. In such cases, we say that the event has a probability, and the probability is equal to the (nearly) common value of the relative frequencies computed from very long sequences of repetitions. Notice that the concept of probability is defined here only for events associated with experiments that, at least in theory, can be repeated many times. Here, repetition of an experiment means repetition with the same circumstances.

To illustrate the situation discussed above, assume the experiment is to select a person and to ask for which candidate he or she would vote if elections were held next Sunday. If a pollster interviews 2,000 people, that is a sequence of 2,000 repetitions of the experiment. The pollster has competitors, and each of them interviews a sample of people; that is, each of them produces a sequence of repetitions of the experiment. If the pollsters are using essentially the same methodology, they repeat the same experiment. The sequences may be of equal or unequal lengths (equal or unequal sample sizes). Each pollster computes the relative frequency of those who say they would vote for a given candidate and uses this value as an estimate of the fraction of votes the candidate would receive. Can one assume that a long-enough sequence (large-enough sample size) exists, however close an estimate is required? Not if the pollsters make errors in selecting their samples. If one selects the sample from upper-class people only and another from middle-class people only, their results may remain different even if both increase their sample sizes. But if their sampling procedure is correct (e.g., every eligible voter has the same chance of being selected), large-enough samples will lead to very close forecasts. This is seen most simply by imagining that the sample sizes become (nearly) as big as the number of those who are eligible to vote. Then, the pollsters will have observations from (essentially) the same samples, and their results will be (nearly) identical. Therefore, in this case, there is a probability associated with the outcomes of the experiment. The argument also shows that the probability of an outcome is equal to the population fraction of the outcome (that is, the fraction of those who, if asked, say they would vote for the given candidate). In other words, with an appropriate sampling procedure, large-enough sample sizes yield arbitrarily precise estimates. Notice, however, that stability of the relative frequencies in the foregoing example usually occurs for sample sizes much smaller than the size of the population. The assumption of the sample sizes getting close to the population size was used only to demonstrate that stability occurs for large-enough samples. To find out how large the samples would have to be for a particular degree of precision in the estimates requires a more involved argument, which will not be presented here. In most countries, pollsters get estimates fairly close to each other and, as it turns out on election day, also close to the true value, using samples in the range of a couple thousand people.

The relationship between probability and relative frequency can be given two different, but related, interpretations. The probabilities are constant quantities, that is, their values do not change from one sequence of repetitions to another. But if the sequences are long enough, the relative frequencies yielded by them will be close to the probability. In this sense, the probability determines—not exactly, but for long sequences, approximately—the relative frequency. On the other hand, the probabilities are rarely known in practice. For example, the population fraction of those intending to vote for a given candidate is never known before the election (if it were known, nobody would be interested in conducting a poll). Therefore, relative frequencies computed from sufficiently large sequences of repetitions (samples) provide the researcher with information regarding the value of the probability. Although, in reality, the probability ought to exist before relative frequencies can be computed, from a practical point of view, observations regarding relative frequencies reveal the value of the probability.

When the experiment does not possess the stability discussed above, our theory does not provide a probability for that case. However, it would be difficult to create an example within the social sciences describing a survey with an appropriately selected sample when this stability does not hold; thus, this is not a serious limitation. A more serious limitation of this theory is that before the question of stability of relative frequencies over long sequences of repetitions can be raised, the experiment needs to be repeated several times. As the experiment involves standardized observations (that is, it also contains the conditions of observation), the theory presented here applies only to situations in which the experiment can be repeated many (maybe very many) times under essentially the same conditions.

Of course, the assumption that an experiment may be repeated very many times under the same conditions is a theoretical assumption, and probability theory has many practical applications in situations when the number of possible replications is limited, or even very small. For example, although this does not fit into the above framework, social scientists may want to associate probabilities with the presidential reelection example. In such cases, probabilistic arguments are used to describe uncertainty, and probability has a somewhat different meaning from the one outlined above.

For example, a student may associate probability with passing an examination: When he or she is better prepared in comparison with the difficulty of the material, the probability of receiving a passing grade is higher. Clearly, in this case, the situation is unique. Even an eventual make-up exam would involve substantially different circumstances. Therefore, the above theory, based on repetitions of an experiment, does not apply. These probabilities can be compared across different exams taken by the same student but may not be comparable across different students. Such probabilities are called *subjective probabilities* because they depend heavily on the judgment of the actual person. There are scientific theories that incorporate these probabilities, but they will not be discussed here. For a modern account of subjective probability and how it can be used in statistics, see Cooke (1991) and Lad (1996). When applied to problems related to sampling and data analysis in the social sciences, these theories lead to the same analyses and conclusions as the frequentist theory presented here. Such a subjective probability is often described by the term *chance,* although sometimes, this word is used interchangeably with the word *probability.*

2.3 Relative Frequencies

Relative frequencies have a number of straightforward properties that carry over to probabilities, and these are studied in the present section.

Property 1. A relative frequency is always between zero and one. In other words, relative frequencies are non-negative numbers, less than one. The relative frequency of an event was defined as the ratio of the number of repetitions of the experiment when the event occurred to the number of times the experiment was repeated. It is quite possible that none of the actual repetitions results in the event in question, and in that case, the frequency of the event (the number of times it occurred) is zero. If a survey is conducted in a neighborhood to determine the preferred location of a bus stop, with four possible choices—say, A, B, C, and D—and 52 people choose A, 17 choose B, none chooses C, and 61 choose D, then the frequency, and also the relative frequency, of location C is zero. No smaller relative frequency can occur. The relative frequency of A is 52/130. If all of the 130 individuals had chosen D, its relative frequency would be $130/130 = 1$, and this is the highest possible value of a relative frequency. To develop a notation for this property, let A denote an arbitrary event and $r(A)$ its relative frequency. Notice that if $f(A)$ is the frequency of event A out of n repetitions of the experiment, then

$$r(A) = f(A)/n.$$

Thus, the property discussed in this paragraph can be written as

$$1 \geq r(A) \geq 0. \qquad \text{Property 1}$$

Property 2. The relative frequency of the opposite of an event is one minus the relative frequency of the original event. The *opposite* of an event is an event that occurs whenever the first event does not occur. If the event in question is choosing location A for the bus stop, its opposite is not voting for A, that is, choosing B or C or D (assuming everybody has a preference). The opposite of A is denoted by A^C (referring to the complement of A). If the experiment is repeated n times and A occurs $f(A)$ times, then in the remaining $n - f(A)$ repetitions of the experiment, A^C occurs. Therefore, $f(A^C) = n - f(A)$. To obtain the relative frequency, one must divide the frequency by the number of times the experiment was repeated. By dividing the previous equation by n, one obtains the following:

$$f(A^C)/n = (n - f(A))/n,$$

which simplifies to

$$r(A^C) = 1 - r(A). \qquad \text{Property 2}$$

Property 3. The relative frequency of a certain event is one. An event is called *certain* if it always occurs. Discussing such events may appear somewhat artificial, but the introduction of this concept will prove to be helpful later. Generally, two events are considered identical if they always occur (or do not occur) together. In this aspect, two certain events cannot be distinguished, and therefore, the existence of only one certain event is assumed. For example, the collection of *all* outcomes of an experiment is the certain event. The certain event is denoted by S (to refer to the fact that it occurs *surely*). As S occurs in every repetition of the experiment, its frequency is n, if the experiment is repeated n times. In notation,

$$f(S) = n.$$

If both sides are divided by n, one obtains the following:

$$r(S) = 1. \qquad \text{Property 3}$$

As a counterpart of S, sometimes the so-called impossible event is a useful concept. This is the event that never occurs, and there exists only one such event. This event can be denoted by 0. The notation refers to the fact that its frequency is zero and, therefore, its relative frequency is also zero: $r(0) = 0$. By definition, the opposite of S is 0 and the opposite of 0 is S (that is, $S^C = 0$ and $0^C = S$), or they are opposite to each other.

Property 4. If two events cannot occur at the same time, then the relative frequency of one of them occurring is the sum of their respective relative frequencies. Two events that cannot occur at the same time are called *disjoint* or *nonoverlapping*. Two outcomes of an experiment are always disjoint. An event and its opposite are always disjoint. If one thinks of an event as the collection of certain outcomes, then two events are disjoint if they do not contain the same outcome. On the other hand, two events occur at the same time if the actual outcome of the experiment is contained in both. If, in research on customer behavior, the experiment is observing which goods, out of a list of, say, eight different products, a customer buys at a grocery store, then this experiment has many outcomes. Every possible collection of goods is an outcome of the experiment. There are, in fact, 256 different baskets possible and all these are separate outcomes of the experiment. If, however, two shoppers buy exactly the same goods out of this list but combine these with other goods not on the list, then the researcher observes the same outcome for these two customers. Notice that this experiment is very different from one in which, with the same products, the first item bought by the customer is observed. That experiment has eight different outcomes.

Depending on the relevant characteristics of the products investigated, there may be different events of interest. The products may be five different brands, A, B, C, D, and E. They all come in regular size, but Brands C, D, and E are available in large size as well. A regular pack of Brand A will be denoted as Ar, a large pack of C as Cl, and so on. Furthermore, assume that Brands A and B are produced by Company X, and Brands C, D, and E are produced by Company Y. (A summary of this example is given in Appendix A.) An event associated with this experiment is that the customer buys a product of Company X. This event occurs whenever the shopper buys one or more of Brands A and B, whether or not other products are being bought at the same time. Another event is that the customer buys a regular pack. This occurs if the basket of goods contains any from among Ar, Br, Cr, Dr, or Er (and possibly other goods). These two events are not disjoint, because they both occur if the customer buys Ar or Br or both. Another event is that the customer buys only brands of Company Y. This occurs when the basket contains goods from among Cr, Cl, Dr, Dl, Er, and El (in any combination), but does not contain any of Ar or Br. This event is disjoint from the first event (buying anything from Company X).

Two events are disjoint if it is impossible for them to occur at the same time. If the event buying a product from X is denoted as (X), and the event buying anything in large size is denoted as (large), the event that they both occur is usually denoted as (X)(large) and is called the *intersection* or *product* of these two events. (Sometimes, we will drop parentheses when writing the product of two events, as in using EF to denote the product of events E and F.) This is, in fact, an operation that has many of the properties of intersections of sets or products of numbers, but this aspect will not be investigated here. Because X does not have products in large size, this fact can be described using the impossible event 0, as (X)(large) = 0.

Now let us consider the relative frequencies of events (X) and (large). In any repetition of the experiment, either (X), or (large), or neither of them occurs, but they cannot both occur at the same time. Considering only repetitions in which one of them occurs, these can be divided into occasions when only (X) occurs and occasions when only (large) occurs. The sum of the frequencies of each of these is equal to the frequency of one of them occurring. The latter event is usually denoted as (X) + (large), implying

$$f(X) + f(large) = f((X) + (large)).$$

Notice that the *sum* of events, more precisely, means that at least one of them occurs, but in the case of disjoint events, which cannot occur together, it is equivalent to one of them occurring. If both sides of the above equation are divided by the number of repetitions, one obtains Property 4. In a less particular notation, let E and F denote two events associated with an experiment.

$$\text{If } EF = 0, \text{ then } r(E) + r(F) = r(E + F). \qquad \text{Property 4}$$

Property 5. The relative frequency of the sum of two events is equal to the sum of their relative frequencies minus the relative frequency of their product. This property generalizes Property 4 and, if the condition of that property holds, yields the same result. Using the previous notation, Property 5 says that

$$r(E + F) = r(E) + r(F) - r(EF). \qquad \text{Property 5}$$

If E and F are disjoint, that is, $EF = 0$, then $r(EF) = r(0) = 0$, and one obtains Property 4.

To see that Property 5 is true, consider events E and F that may occur together. For example, let (B,C,D) denote the event that the customer buys any from B, C, and D. Then,

$$(B,C,D)(\text{large}) = (Cl, Dl),$$

as can be seen from Figure 2.1. Figure 2.1 is a Venn diagram, where circles represent events.

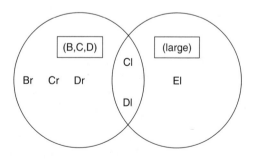

Figure 2.1   Intersection of Events (B, C, D) and (large) in the Customer Behavior Example

With respect to events (B,C,D) and (large), all repetitions of the experiment belong in one and only one category of the following list:

Both (B,C,D) and (large) occurred.
Only (B,C,D) occurred, and (large) did not occur.
Only (large) occurred, and (B,C,D) did not occur.
Neither (B,C,D) nor (large) occurred.

These possibilities are combinations of events and are events themselves. The following list contains the same events using the complement and product notations:

$$(B,C,D)(large)$$

$$(B,C,D)(large)^C$$

$$(B,C,D)^C(large)$$

$$(B,C,D)^C(large)^C$$

It is clear that these four events are pairwise disjoint, that is, they cannot occur together, not even two of them. At least one of (B,C,D) and (large) occurs if exactly one of them or both occur. In notation:

$$(B,C,D) + (large) = (B,C,D)(large) + (B,C,D)(large)^C \\ + (B,C,D)^C(large).$$

Obviously,

$$(B,C,D)(large) + (B,C,D)(large)^C = (B,C,D)$$

and

$$(B,C,D)(large) + (B,C,D)^C(large) = (large).$$

The first of the above equations simply reads that the shopper buys from B, C, D if at least one product from B, C, D is bought, regardless of whether there is one in large size. The second equation reads that a product in large size is bought if that happens, whether or not that product is from among B, C, D. Property 4 may then be applied, yielding that

$$r((B,C,D)(large)) + r((B,C,D)(large)^C) = r(B,C,D)$$

and

$$r((B,C,D)(large)) + r((B,C,D)^C(large)) = r(large).$$

A combination of the foregoing results yields the following:

$$r((B,C,D) + (large)) = r(B,C,D) + r((B,C,D)^C(large)) =$$

$$r((B,C,D)(large) + (B,C,D)(large)^C + (B,C,D)^C(large)) =$$

$$r(B,C,D) + r(large) - r((B,C,D)(large)),$$

which is exactly Property 5. An intuitive explanation of this property is that $r((B,C,D) + (large))$ is less than $r(B,C,D) + r(large)$, because the latter sum contains the relative frequency of the intersection, that is, $r((A,B,C)(large))$, twice.

The properties of relative frequencies are summarized in Appendix B.

2.4 Experiments With Infinitely Many Outcomes

The theory developed so far works well to describe observations with a limited number of outcomes, like customers' choice from the available products or answers to questions concerning the personal characteristics of the respondents to a questionnaire, such as gender, educational level, employment status, and so on. In the social sciences, data of a somewhat different nature are often collected, and the theory needs further development in order to be able to describe such situations. An important example of this somewhat different kind of data is information collected on the incomes of respondents.

One obvious difference is that, whereas the number of different responses concerning, for example, employment status is limited to a relatively small number of options, in the case of income, the number of possible responses is very large. It would be difficult to give a realistic upper limit for annual income. More importantly, there is a well-defined and relevant difference between, say, not being employed because of retirement or because of not being able to find a job (people in the former category are not considered as unemployed and are not taken into account when the unemployment rate is calculated, whereas people in the latter category are). With the income question, the difference between, say, $35,510 and $35,520 as a yearly income is clear but not very important. A difference of $10 per year will not lead to appreciable differences in the material well-being of the respective respondents. Moreover, such responses are often subject to error, and therefore, it is difficult to know whether the incomes of the two respondents really are different. Relative frequencies are not particularly useful, because if the values are reported precisely enough, most of the figures will be mentioned only once and the frequencies will be one. Consequently, for large samples, the relative frequencies mostly will be close to zero (one divided by the sample size). It may very well be the case that both $55,350 and $250,000 are mentioned once, and the relative frequency will not tell the researcher that incomes in the range of $40,000 to $60,000 occur far more frequently than incomes in the range of $240,000 to $260,000. Therefore, assigning frequencies to intervals is more useful in such cases than assigning frequencies to individual observations.

For these reasons, rather than the individual figures, the distributions of those figures in certain intervals are of primary interest. These brackets are often defined in advance, and respondents are asked to mark the interval into which their incomes fall. Because no theoretical maximum of possible incomes is known, the last interval, in fact, has to be a half line (all incomes higher than a certain threshold). With data collected this way, even the determination of such simple statistics as the mean is difficult. The theoretically sound solution for handling experiments with very many numerical outcomes relies on intervals instead of too many different numerical values. Not a few intervals defined in advance, but rather an approach that makes it possible to determine the (relative) frequency of any interval on the number line.

The assumption that we make here may appear to further complicate the situation. However, it will, in fact, turn out to be a great simplification. It is assumed that all numbers (including, sometimes, even negative numbers) are possible outcomes. This assumption would make it quite impossible to think about the relative frequencies of all possible observations (every number). Of course, the frequencies or relative frequencies of those values actually observed could be computed, but, as discussed above, these values may not be informative. What is feasible, even after this assumption has been made, is to consider the relative frequencies of intervals. It will be shown now that this is both possible and helpful in describing the behavior of the experiment.

Even if one concentrates on intervals, there are infinitely many of them. It is possible that one has infinitely many intervals, and that all have positive numbers associated with them that sum to one. To interpret these numbers as relative frequencies, one would have to disregard the limitations set by the sample size. Therefore, as will be done in the next chapter, considering the values as probabilities is more realistic. The immediate goal here is to illustrate that such numbers do exist. For example, consider the intervals $(-1, 0)$ and $[0, 1)$. The notation here implies that zero is contained in

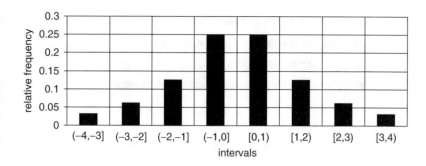

Figure 2.2   Relative Frequencies That Can Be Extended to Infinitely Many Intervals: An Example

the second interval but not in the first. Next, consider the two intervals $(-2, -1]$ and $[1, 2)$. Then, consider $(-3, -2]$ and $[2, 3)$, and so on. These intervals together cover the entire line and are pairwise disjoint. To be able to give a correct description of experiments with infinitely many outcomes, by the properties discussed in the previous section, their respective relative frequencies ought to sum to one, if one could define the meaning of the sum of infinitely many numbers. In fact, this can be done, for example, if the relative frequencies of the intervals are as shown in Figure 2.2. The relative frequencies of the first two intervals $((-1, 0)$ and $[0, 1))$ are 0.25. The relative frequencies of the next two intervals $((-2, 1]$ and $[1, 2))$ are 0.125, that is, half of the previous value, and the relative frequencies of the next two $((-3, -2]$ and $[2, 3))$ are 0.0625, that is, half of the previous value. This assignment can be continued: An interval always has a relative frequency equal to one half of that of the interval next to it, closer to zero. By this assignment, all intervals have positive relative frequencies (no value, however large it may be, is excluded from the potential observations). The sum of the relative frequencies of the first two intervals is $0.25 + 0.25 = 0.5$. The sum of the first four intervals adds $0.125 + 0.125 = 0.25$ to this, that is, $0.5 + 0.25 = 0.75$. Similarly, the sum of the first six relative frequencies is $0.5 + 0.25 + 0.125 = 0.875$, and the sum of the relative frequencies of the first eight intervals is $0.5 + 0.25 + 0.125 + 0.0625 = 0.9375$, and so on. Thus, summation can be continued, always using the sum of finitely many numbers. It will never reach one (the remaining value is always halved), but after having taken into account a large enough number of intervals, it can get arbitrarily close to one. This can be proved mathematically, but it can also be seen intuitively: By adding the sum of the relative frequencies of the next two intervals, the sum will be "halfway" closer to one. For example,

18

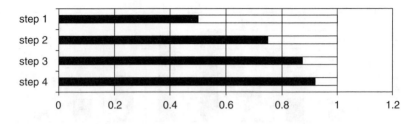

Figure 2.3   The Sum of Infinitely Many Positive Numbers May Be 1

having summed the relative frequencies of the first four cells, the sum is $1/2 + 1/4 = 3/4$, that is, $1 - 3/4 = 1/4$ away from one. Half of this distance is $1/8$, and the next sum (the sum of the relative frequencies of the first six intervals) is $1/2 + 1/4 + 1/8$, which is also equal to $3/4 + 1/8$, that is, "halfway" closer to one than the previous sum was. This is illustrated in Figure 2.3.

There may, of course, be other relative frequencies (or probabilities) associated with the intervals with the property that they sum to one. Another straightforward example is $0.9 + 0.09 + 0.009 + 0.0009 + \ldots = 0.9999\ldots = 1$. More efficient ways of thinking about relative frequencies (and probabilities) with this property will be discussed later.

We have seen that infinitely many intervals may have positive relative frequencies that sum to one, but are such relative frequencies useful in understanding the probabilities behind the experiment? First, such relative frequencies may not be estimated from samples of finite sizes. This difficulty could be overcome by assuming that, outside of some thresholds, the relative frequencies are zero. But one does not want to choose this option because it would be identical to defining thresholds, which we wanted to avoid in the first place. The other solution would be not to estimate the relative frequencies separately, but rather to assume that the relative frequencies of the different intervals are related to each other by some function, and in this case, only the parameters of that function would have to be estimated. As will be discussed later, such functions may be defined, and more importantly, they are not merely fictitious constructions but actually exist—with good approximation—in practice. One celebrated example is the so-called normal distribution, to be considered in Chapter 4. Second, relative frequencies (and the underlying probabilities) can be associated with any interval, however small it may be, and the intervals can be combined with each other. In fact, when infinitely many different (numerical) outcomes of an experiment are considered, the intervals are the events, and knowing the relative frequency or probability of every interval gives a complete description of the experiment.

3. PROPERTIES OF PROBABILITY

Because probabilities are theoretical and directly unobservable quantities that govern the relative frequencies that one can observe, it is reasonable to assume that some of the properties of relative frequencies are shared by probabilities. For example, if a probability could be larger than 1, say 1.1, then how would it be possible that the relative frequency from a long-enough repetition of the experiment could get arbitrarily close to it, given that a relative frequency never exceeds 1? By the same argument, several properties of probability can be established.

3.1 Basic Properties

If the value of the relative frequency of an event approximates arbitrarily well the probability of that event, one obtains properties of probability by replacing the relative frequency of an event by its probability. Let $P(E)$ denote the probability of event E. Notice that this probability depends on the experiment considered. The same event may occur in different experiments with different probabilities. For example, the probability of seeing a rainbow is different if observations are made after rain and if observations are made after rain when the sun is shining. As we all know, the relative frequency, and, therefore, the probability of a rainbow is higher in the second experiment than in the first one. This dependence of the probability on the experiment will, however, be suppressed in the notation. All events considered are assumed to be associated with the same experiment, and it will be mentioned explicitly when this is not the case. Remember that outcomes are also events, and the events are certain combinations of outcomes. Two events are identical if they always occur together. Therefore, to define an event, it is sufficient to determine when it does and does not occur.

The first property of relative frequencies implies that

$$1 \geq P(E) \geq 0$$

for all events E. The opposite of E is denoted by E^C, and the second property of relative frequencies implies that

$$P(E^C) = 1 - P(E)$$

for all events E. By Property 3, the probabilities of the certain and impossible events are given as

$$P(S) = 1, P(0) = 0.$$

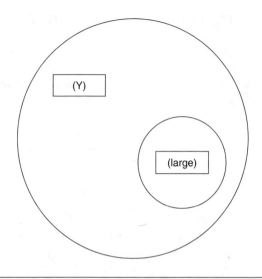

Figure 3.1   The Event (large) Implies the Event (Y)

The fourth property implies that if EF = 0, then

$$P(E) + P(F) = P(E + F),$$

where the sum of two events means that at least one of them occurs. This property, to be discussed further in the next section, has important consequences.

We say that an event implies another one if the second event occurs in all repetitions of the experiment when the first one occurred. In the customer behavior example, (large) implies (Y), because large size is available for brands C, D, and E only, and these are produced by Company Y. On the other hand, (Y) does not imply (large), because one can buy a product of Company Y without buying something in large size—Cr, for example. Implications among events may be graphically illustrated: If an event is implied by another one, the circle associated with the implied event in a Venn diagram is drawn to contain the circle associated with the implying event. This is illustrated for the events (large) and (Y) in Figure 3.1. Here, the shape (circle) has no particular meaning—only the relationship between the two circles (one is contained in the other one) is meaningful. Venn diagrams may also be used to illustrate more general relationships between two or more events.

The fact that (large) implies (Y) is denoted as (large) $\subseteq$ (Y) or (Y) $\supseteq$ (large). This notation is borrowed from set theory and refers to the fact that the outcomes that are contained in (large), namely Cl, Dl, and El, are a subset of the outcomes contained in (Y), namely Cr, Cl, Dr, Dl, Er, and El. This also points to another way of looking at this relationship. An event is a collection of outcomes, and after having observed a particular outcome of the experiment, all the events containing this outcome are said to have occurred. An event implies another one if any outcome that belongs to it also belongs to the other event.

As one would expect, if E implies F and F implies E, then the two events are the same. In fact, if all outcomes belonging to E also belong to F, and all outcomes belonging to F also belong to E, then the two sets of outcomes are identical and the two events occur at the same time. In terms of a Venn diagram, each circle contains the other one; therefore, they are identical.

If $E \subseteq F$, then the occurrences of F can be divided into two groups: occasions when E also occurred and occasions when E did not occur, that is, when E^C occurred. The first situation can be described as EF and the second one as $E^C F$. Then,

$$F = EF + E^C F,$$

because in all cases when F occurs, E does or does not occur and there is no other possibility. The same fact was discussed for F = (large) and E = (B,C,D) at the end of Section 2.3. This is a decomposition of F and is illustrated with a Venn diagram in Figure 3.2. The events EF and $E^C F$ are disjoint, because E occurred in the first event and that it did not in the second event, and therefore, there is no outcome that would be contained in both EF and $E^C F$. This implies that

$$P(F) = P(EF) + P(E^C F).$$

Furthermore, if $E \subseteq F$, then

$$EF = E.$$

To see this, notice that equality of two events means that they occur at the same time (and also do not occur at the same time), and therefore, it is enough to realize that EF occurs exactly when E does. But this is easy: If EF occurs, then both E and F occur, therefore E also occurs; if E occurs, it implies F and therefore both E and F occur; that is, EF occurs. Thus, the previous equation for the probabilities can be written as

$$P(F) = P(E) + P(E^C F).$$

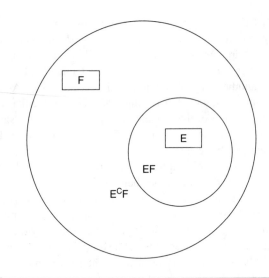

Figure 3.2   E Implies F—With Decomposition of F Denoted

Taking into account that probabilities are non-negative numbers, one obtains that

$$P(F) \geq P(E), \text{ if } F \supseteq E.$$

It should be emphasized that the foregoing argument showed that if $E \subseteq F$, then $EF = E$. Similarly, if $E \subseteq F$, then $E + F = F$. This also implies that $ES = E$ and $E + 0 = E$ for all events E.

When $E \subseteq F$, then if E occurs, F also occurs. In this case, if E occurs, then no uncertainty remains with respect to the occurrence of F. For any two events E and F, one may be interested in seeing whether the occurrence of E influences the probability of F. One may define a probability for the occurrence of F for the cases when E also occurred. This quantity may be different from the overall (disregarding whether or not E occurred) probability of F. The probability of F when E occurred is called the conditional probability of F, given E, and is denoted by P(F|E). To develop the concept of the conditional probability, consider first the relative frequency of F. For a large number of repetitions of the experiment, this is a good approximation of the probability of F. Then consider those cases only, when E occurred. The number of these cases is f(E). Out of these, the frequency of F is the number of those cases when both E and F occurred, f(EF). The relative frequency of F out of the cases when E also occurred is f(EF)/f(E). This is the conditional relative frequency of F, given E. By analogy with the relationship between relative frequency and probability, the conditional probability of F, given E, is defined as

$$P(F|E) = P(EF)/P(E),$$

or as the ratio of the joint probability to the probability of the condition.

Two events are said to be *independent* if the probability that both occur is the product of their respective probabilities. That is, E and F are independent if

$$P(EF) = P(E)P(F).$$

Note that whether or not two events are independent is not a property of the two events only, but also of their probabilities, which may be different in different experiments. In the customer behavior example, suppose that $P(B,C,D) = 0.4$, $P(large) = 0.6$, and $P(Cl,Dl) = 0.24$. In this case, (B,C,D) and (large) are independent. An interpretation of this fact is that if 60% of all customers buy a large product, then also 60% of those who buy at least one from B, C, and D buy a large one. If $P(B,C,D) = 0.5$, $P(large) = 0.4$, and $P(Cl,Dl) = 0.3$, then (B,C,D) and (large) are not independent because 40% of all customers buy a large product, but from among those who buy at least one from B, C, and D, it is not 40% who buy a large product. If (B,C,D) and (large) were independent, $P(Cl,Dl)$ would be 0.2 in this case, but it is 0.3. Among those who buy at least one from B, C, and D, a larger fraction buys a large product than from the general population, and the two events are not independent.

If two events E and F are independent, then the conditional probability of F, given E, is the same as the (unconditional) probability of F:

$$P(F|E) = P(EF)/P(E) = (P(E)P(F))/P(E) = P(F).$$

This means that if E and F are independent, then knowing that E occurred does not influence the probability of F. Also, in this case, the occurrence of F does not influence the probability of E, $P(E|F) = P(E)$. Moreover, $P(F|E) = P(F)$ implies that E and F are independent; so does $P(E|F) = P(E)$. Therefore, the independence of two events is equivalent to the conditional probability of either one of them, given the other one, being equal to the unconditional probability.

The concept of independence, as described above, is a fairly good approximation of independence as it is understood in everyday language. One important application of independence is in sampling, where the sample units have to be selected independently of each other. This is usually understood as the requirement that selecting a person into the sample should not influence the chances of another person being selected into the sample. For example, in a sampling procedure, if households are first selected and then every member of the chosen households is selected into the sample, the independence requirement is violated. Independence in the sample selection procedure is frequently implemented by barring information concerning the selection of a certain person into the sample from the phase when the decision about selecting or not selecting another person into the sample is made.

Independence extends to more than two events. The events E, F, and G are independent if $P(E,F,G) = P(E)P(F)P(G)$. If k events, each with probability p, are independent, then the probability of their product (the event that all of them occurred) is p^k.

3.2 Additivity

For events E and F (not necessarily disjoint), Property 5 implies that

$$P(E + F) = P(F) + P(E) - P(EF).$$

This simple rule extends to several events, and the complexity of the formula depends on the relationships among the events involved. For example, if the probabilities $P(X)$, $P(large)$, and $P(D)$ are given, one may be interested in finding out the probability of $(X) + (large) + (D)$. This is an event, and it means that someone buys a product from X or buys any product in large size or buys Product D in any size, or any combination of these. If a person buys Ar, the event occurs; if a person buys Cs only, the event does not occur. To obtain the relevant probability, the different combinations of the events that may occur need to be evaluated. The sum of these three events may occur so that exactly one of them occurs, or so that exactly two of them occur, or so that all three occur at the same time. The first possibility means that any of the following occurs:

$$(X)((large)^C)(D^C)$$

$$(X^C)(large)(D^C)$$

$$(X^C)((large)^C)(D).$$

The second situation, that is, when exactly two of them occur, means either one of the following:

$$(X)(large)(D^C)$$

$$(X)((\text{large})^C)(D)$$

$$(X^C)(\text{large})(D).$$

The third situation means that

$$(X)(\text{large})(D).$$

These seven events cover all possibilities, and one can say that

$$(X) + (\text{large}) + (D) = (X)((\text{large}^C))(D^C) + (X^C)(\text{large})(D^C) + (X^C)$$
$$((\text{large})^C)(D) + (X)(\text{large})(D^C) + (X)((\text{large})^C)(D)$$
$$+ (X^C)(\text{large})(D) + (X)(\text{large})(D).$$

An important property of these seven events is that they are pairwise disjoint. These combinations are illustrated for the three events E, F, and G in Figure 3.3. The sum of them, $E + F + G$, is the area they cover jointly, and the various possibilities are shown as intersections of the original events and/or their complements.

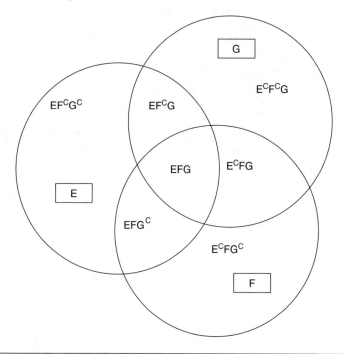

Figure 3.3   Relative Positions of Three Events E, F, G

The formula for the probability of the sum of three events is obtained as follows. First, notice that

$$P((X) + (large) + (D)) = P((X) + (large)) + P(D) - P(((X) + (large))(D)),$$

and this can be written further as

$$P((X) + (large) + (D)) = P(X) +$$
$$P(large) + P(D) - P((X)(large)) - P(((X) + (large))(D)),$$

using Property 5. Then, consider the event $((X) + (large))(D)$. It means that $(X) + (large)$ occurs, and also (D) occurs. In other words, it means that a product of Company X or a product in large size or both is being bought, and Product D is also being purchased. This means that either a product of X and D is being purchased, or a product in large size and D is being bought, or both. This is exactly the event $(X)(D) + (large)(D)$. Using Property 5, again, one obtains

$$P(((X) + (large))(D)) = P((X)(D) + (large)(D)) = P((X)(D)) + P((large)(D)) -$$
$$P(((X)(D))((large)(D))).$$

Here, obviously, $((X)(D))((large)(D)) = ((X)(large)(D))$. A combination of the previous results yields

$$P((X) + (large) + (D)) = P(X) + P(large) + P(D) - P((X)(large)) -$$
$$P((X)(D)) - P((large)(D)) + P((X)(large)(D)).$$

In words, the result says that the probability of the sum of three events is the sum of the probabilities of the original events, minus the probabilities of the pairwise products, plus the probability of the product of the three events. Notice that in the case of the present example, $((X)(large)(D)) = 0$, and therefore its probability is zero, because Company X does not have a product in large size.

The foregoing argument is well illustrated by Figure 3.3. In this figure, area plays a role similar to probability, and the probability of the sum of the three events is the area covered by them. But the pairwise intersections are covered twice, and the intersection of all three is covered three times. The above formula is parallel to the one that could be used to compute the area covered by the three circles, using the respective areas of the circles and their intersections. Notice that the relationship between probability and area is much deeper than this illustration shows. Aspects of this deeper connection will be outlined and used later.

3.3 Density Functions

The main goal of the present section is to describe how probability can be defined when, rather than considering only experiments with finitely many outcomes, experiments with infinitely many outcomes are considered, and to introduce the most important tools for handling such situations.

In the previous chapter, some of the reasons behind considering experiments with infinitely many outcomes were considered. To further motivate the development in this section, another example is mentioned briefly. One of the most frequent applications of probability theory by social scientists is formulating assumptions (statistical hypotheses) and using data to judge how realistic these assumptions may be. A test of a statistical hypothesis is usually carried out (see Henkel, 1976) by computing the value of some test statistic and judging how frequently (or with what probability) values more extreme than the actual value occur, if the hypothesis is true. If such values are too unlikely, the hypothesis is rejected. Therefore, the determination of the distribution of the test statistic is of primary importance. The value of the test statistic depends on the actual sample: Even for relatively small sample sizes, it may have so many different values, depending on the actual observations, that it is more manageable to assume that any value may be observed–that is, one considers an experiment with infinitely many outcomes.

When an experiment with infinitely many outcomes is considered, all of the previous results remain valid, but one is also confronted with new questions. The first of these is the definition of the operations sum and product for the case of infinitely many events (obviously, when the experiment has finitely many outcomes, the number of events is also finite, and when the number of outcomes is infinite, the number of events is also infinite).

The product and the sum of infinitely many events can be defined just as in the case of two events. In the previous section, the straightforward extension of these operations to three events was discussed, and the extension to a larger number of events follows the same line. The product of infinitely many events is the event that occurs if all the original events occur, and the sum of infinitely many events is the event that occurs if (at least) one of the original events occurs.

But how can probabilities be associated with the outcomes and events if there are infinitely many of them? In this section, a convenient method of associating probabilities with the intervals on the number line is discussed. This method will be very useful when the outcomes of the experiment are real numbers.

The most common way of associating probabilities with intervals is to consider a positive and continuous function. It is assumed that the total area

28

Figure 3.4   A Density Function. The area under the curve is equal to 1.

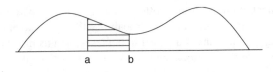

Figure 3.5   The Probability of an Interval

under the function is equal to 1. Such a function is called a *density function*. Figure 3.4 shows an example of a density function.

A density function indicates the probability of any interval on the number line. More precisely, the density function indicates, for every interval, the probability of observing a value that falls into this interval. To obtain the probability of an interval, one simply has to take the area under the curve within the interval. This is illustrated in Figure 3.5. The probability of having an observation in the interval (a,b), that is, of observing a value between a and b, is equal to the shaded area.

When one shifts the interval over the number line, its probability changes depending on the density function. If one moves the interval to the right, its probability first decreases, then increases, and then decreases again. The probability of any interval where the density function is zero over the entire interval is zero as well.

Probabilities are assumed to govern frequencies after a large number of repetitions of the experiment have been observed, so that the relative frequencies are close to the probabilities. This implies that the frequency of observations is small in an interval where the density function takes on small values, and the frequency is large where the density function is large. More precisely, if two intervals of the same length are considered, one expects more observations in the one where the density function is greater and fewer observations in the one where the density function is smaller. Therefore, the observations occur more densely in intervals where the density function is higher. The density function shows the expected density of observations, as illustrated in Figure 3.6. Observations in interval (a,b) occur more frequently than observations in interval (c,d).

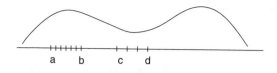

Figure 3.6   The Density Function Shows the Expected Density of Observations

On the other hand, when observations are available on the number line, histograms are often drawn to summarize the distribution of the data (see Jacoby, 1997). If the histogram is based on intervals of the same length, as is usually the case, an interval with a higher frequency will have a higher bar on it than an interval with a lower frequency. Therefore, the properties of the data can be read from a histogram similarly to the way the density function describes the probabilities of the intervals. In fact, histograms can be used to approximate density functions just as relative frequencies approximate probabilities. If the number of observations increases and the length of the intervals on the histograms decreases, the histogram becomes finer and finer and approximates the density function better and better. To illustrate this process, 1,000 observations were generated from a certain density function. Figure 3.7 contains histograms based on the first 100, the first 500, and all the 1,000 observations, respectively. To draw the histograms, 11, 22, and 31 groups were used, respectively. Consequently, the length of the intervals becomes smaller for larger sample sizes. It can be seen that the histograms become smoother as the number of observations increases. In fact, the observations have been generated from the density shown in Figure 3.8. This is the density of a normal distribution (to be discussed in Section 4.4). The similarity between the last histogram in Figure 3.7 and the density in Figure 3.8 is clear. Notice that the property that the histograms approximate the density function is not restricted to particular types of distributions.

It is easy to see that probabilities defined using a density possess the properties of probability discussed earlier. The areas are non-negative numbers, and if an interval contains another one, the probability assigned to the former cannot be less than the probability associated with the latter. The additivity property also holds true, as shown in Figure 3.9. The sum of the intervals (a,b) and (c,d) is the interval (a,d), and its probability (i.e., the area above it) is the sum of the probabilities of (a,b) and of (c,d) minus the probability of the interval (c,b) [i.e., the area above (a,b) plus the area above (c,d) minus the area above (c,b)].

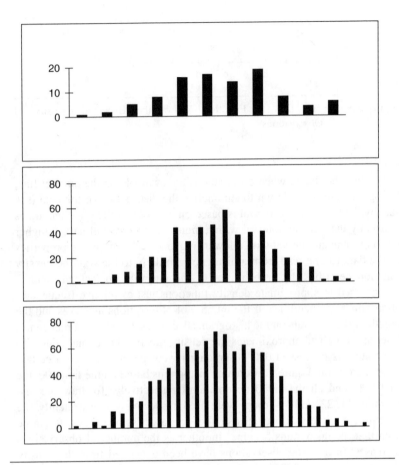

Figure 3.7   Histograms Based on 100, 500 and 1,000 Observations From a Density Function

For arbitrary values of e < f < g, the two intervals (e,f) and (f,g) are adjacent and nonoverlapping, and their sum is the interval (e,g). The probability of the latter interval is the sum of the probabilities of the two original intervals. If one chooses an arbitrary value h, other than f, between e and g, then the interval (e,g) is also the sum of (e,h) and (h,g). But it easily follows from the properties of area that the probability of (e,g), computed from the sum of the probabilities of (e,h) and (h,g), is the same as the probability computed from the sum of probabilities of (e,f) and (f,g). One could also consider intervals that are neither overlapping nor adjacent. Although

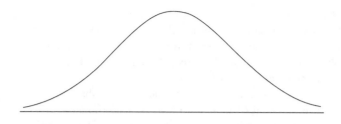

Figure 3.8   The Density Function From Which the Observations in Figure 3.7 Were Taken

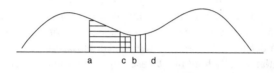

Figure 3.9   The Additivity Rule for the Probability of Intervals

their sum is not an interval, one can assign a probability to it, namely, the sum of the probabilities of the two intervals. This method leads to probabilities of more general sets on the number line, but this will not be pursued here any further.

As described above, density functions assign probabilities to intervals. A value on the number line is an interval of length zero, and the area above it is zero no matter where the number is and no matter what the value of the density function is at that point. Density functions, as defined above, assign zero probability to every point on the number line. However, the points may have different density values. For example, with the density function shown in Figure 3.9, the value a has a higher density than the value d does. This implies that if one considers two small intervals of equal length containing a and d, respectively, for example, $(a-\varepsilon, a+\varepsilon)$ and $(d-\varepsilon, d+\varepsilon)$, where ε is a small positive value, then the probability of $(a-\varepsilon, a+\varepsilon)$ is greater than that of $(d-\varepsilon, d+\varepsilon)$.

3.4 Countable Additivity

After the sum of infinitely many events has been defined, one may be interested in seeing whether the rule about the probability of the sum of events remains true. This question would be relevant, for example, if one wanted to know whether the probability that a value (of an observation or of a test statistic) exceeds a certain value, say 3.5, is equal to the sum of the probabilities of the events, that it is between 3.5 and 4.5, between 4.5 and 5.5, between 5.5 and 6.5, and so on.

For pairwise disjoint events, one would expect that the probability of their sum is the sum of their probabilities. Unfortunately, this cannot be stated with such generality, and the reason behind this is the difficulty associated with defining the sum of infinitely many numbers. Figure 2.1 and the argument in the previous chapter showed that this can be done in an important special case: when the infinitely many numbers to be added can be ordered to form a sequence. This is the case, for example, with the relative frequencies or probabilities of intervals of unit lengths next to each other on the number line. One can have infinitely many numbers in several different ways. When they can be ordered so that they form a sequence, their sum can be defined. (In fact, the values also have to be non-negative, but this will automatically hold in the case of probabilities.) When they cannot be ordered to form a sequence, the sum cannot be defined. An infinite set (numbers or events) is called *countable* if it can be ordered to form a sequence.

If the set of outcomes of an experiment is not countable,[1] the definition of probability has to be altered: It is not the outcomes, but rather certain collections of outcomes (events) have probabilities. For example, if the outcomes are all the numbers on the number line (the so-called real numbers), then all intervals have probabilities. If probabilities for all intervals are given, then, in spite of not being able to associate probabilities with every outcome, by considering small-enough intervals, one has information regarding how likely certain outcomes are. In the previous section, an efficient method of defining the probabilities of all intervals was given. Density functions associate probabilities with intervals on the number line, but they associate the value zero with every point (i.e., number). We say that every outcome has zero probability. This, however, does not imply that observations in small neighborhoods of different points would occur with the same probability. Where the density is higher, observations are more likely to occur. Although the probability of every outcome is zero, we say that they have different *likelihoods*. The likelihood of a given value is equal to the value of the density function (i.e., the height of the curve) at that value. All of the individual numbers occur with probability zero, but they may have different likelihoods. Observations in the vicinity of values with higher likelihoods have higher probabilities than do observations in the vicinity of values with smaller likelihood values.

When countably many pairwise disjoint events are given, the probability of their sum is the sum of their probabilities, which is a direct extension of the similar property for finitely many (e.g., 2) events. Here, the sum of countably many numbers (the probabilities) is understood as the limit of the finite sums, as was illustrated earlier, for example, with the sequence 0.9, 0.09, 0.009, 0.0009, and so on. The finite sums (the sums of the first two, first three, first four, etc., components) are 0.99, 0.999, 0.9999, . . . , respectively, and the value to which these converge is 1 in the present case. In the case of the example in Figure 2.2 (interpreting the values as probabilities rather than relative frequencies), the sum of the intervals on the positive half line is the half line itself (i.e., the event that the observation is positive), and the probability of this event is the limit of the finite sums: 1/4, 3/8, 7/16, 15/32 . . . that is, 1/2. This procedure may also be viewed as an approximation procedure. The half line is approximated by the (finite) sum of the intervals, and, at the same time, its probability is also approximated by the finite sums of their respective probabilities.

To develop a notation for the countable additivity property, let E_1, E_2, E_3, . . . be pairwise disjoint events; that is, $E_i E_j = 0$, for all different pairs i and j. Then,

$$P(E_1 + E_2 + E_3 + \dots) = P(E_1) + P(E_2) + P(E_3) + \dots.$$

The left-hand side of the equation is the probability of the sum of the infinitely many events (i.e., of the event that occurs if at least one of the original events occurs), and the right-hand side is the sum of the probabilities of the original events (i.e., the value to which the finite sums converge).

4. PROBABILITY DISTRIBUTIONS AND RANDOM VARIABLES

To obtain a good summary description of an experiment when using a stochastic model, one has to consider the possible outcomes together with their probabilities. Such a description is appropriate when one has finitely many outcomes and also in the case of infinitely many outcomes if the outcomes are countable. When the outcomes are not countable (as in the case when all real numbers are assumed to be possible outcomes), one has to consider the outcomes not with their probabilities (as these are not informative) but with their likelihoods, that is, the density function. In this chapter, we discuss frequently occurring experiments and the properties of such summary descriptions.

4.1 The Discrete Case

As seen earlier, the intuitive concept of probability works well if the experiment has finitely many outcomes, or infinitely many outcomes when they are countable. These two situations together are usually referred to as the *discrete* case. Experiments with countably many outcomes are important not only as a good approximation of experiments with uncountable outcomes. (A good approximation of the situation with all real numbers as possible outcomes is the assumption that the different outcomes are small intervals next to each other. This approximation is similar to the approximation of the density function by a fine histogram.) Experiments with countably many outcomes are also good approximations of certain data collection procedures.

When data are collected over a specified period of time, but the number of observations is not determined in advance, one cannot determine the number of different possible outcomes. For example, in a survey of reading habits, the sampling procedure may select certain bookstores and determine certain periods of time (e.g., one hour in the morning and one hour in the afternoon, each day the shops are open), and all sales are recorded during these periods. It is difficult to tell in advance what the total number of sales will be, and it is even more difficult to tell what the possible highest number of sales may be. Of course, depending on the number of shops involved, figures like 1 million or 1 billion are practically impossible observations. As an approximation, it will be assumed that any value is possible (but very large values will have such small probabilities that one cannot, in practice, expect them to occur). One should not forget, however, that the values can only be integers. In this case, a good model assumes that the possible outcomes of the experiment are all integers. These are countable, as they are ordered in a natural way.

Depending on the data collection procedure, it may occur in reality that the number of different outcomes is in the range of hundreds of millions. If credit card transactions, e-mail routing events, or visits to home pages belonging to a certain domain name are registered over a period of time, such figures are quite realistic. In such cases, one may also consider dropping the discrete nature of the model and assuming all numbers are observable, not just the integers. Such models will be discussed later in this chapter. The decision regarding the theoretical experiment to describe the actual data collection procedure ought to depend on several factors. Relevant properties of the data collection method should be included in the model, and less important ones may be omitted. Importance has to be judged with respect to the goal of the research. In this respect, the decision is similar to that concerning the application of a deterministic or a stochastic model.

In the rest of this section, only experiments with finitely many outcomes will be considered because the rules for countably many outcomes are essentially the same. A generalization of the material to countably many outcomes would be very similar to the generalization of the additivity property of probabilities of disjoint events to countably many events.

When the experiment has finitely many outcomes, each one of them has a probability, that is, a number associated with it, so that

- the probabilities are all between zero and one
- the sum of all probabilities is one.

The foregoing conditions can be formulated as follows. Let $E_1, E_2, \ldots, E_k$ be the outcomes of an experiment. The numbers $P(E_1) = P_1, P(E_2) = P_2, \ldots,$ $P(E_k) = P_k$ with the properties

$$1 \geq P_i \geq 0, \text{ for all } i = 1, 2, \ldots, k$$

$$P_1 + P_2 + \cdots + P_k = 1$$

are called a finite probability distribution. The word *distribution* refers to the total probability, that is, 1, being distributed among the outcomes. The two properties above ensure that all properties of the probability will be true if the probabilities of events are defined as the sum of the probabilities of the outcomes that they contain. In the countable case, one would have countably many non-negative numbers summing to one. Indeed, Figure 2.3 illustrated that this is possible.

Probability distributions, as collections of numbers with certain properties, can be considered without reference to a particular experiment. It is quite possible that different experiments can be described by the same probability distribution.

One of the simplest finite probability distributions is the so-called *uniform distribution*. Here, every outcome has the same probability. Because the probabilities sum to one, the common value of the probabilities is $1/k$, where k is the number of outcomes of the experiment. If there are two candidates for president of the United States and they are equally popular, or the population of interest contains the same number of men and women, one can use the same model for describing the observation of the preference of a voter or recording the gender of a respondent: The experiment has two outcomes, each having the same probability. Notice, however, that when these elementary steps are repeated, as in sampling from the respective populations, not all outcomes remain equally probable. If a thousand people are interviewed regarding their preference for president, the outcome that 10 of them would choose one candidate and the remaining 990 the other one occurs with much less probability than the outcome that 550 choose one candidate and the remaining 450 the other one if, in the population, the two candidates are equally popular. This fact will be discussed in the next section.

An important feature of uniform distributions is that the probabilities of events can be determined very simply. The probability of an event associated with an experiment with uniform distribution is the sum of the probabilities of the outcomes it contains. Because all the outcomes have probability 1/k, where k is the number of different outcomes, the probability of the event is the number of outcomes it contains divided by the total number of outcomes. For example, if four teams, A, B, C, and D, are participating in a tournament and the schedule of matches is determined by random drawing (i.e., draws with equal chances), the coach of Team A may want to know the probability of them not meeting Team D, their strongest rival, before the last game. To determine this probability, one simply needs to determine the number of different schedules and the number of those when the event occurs. In this case, all possible schedules can be listed as follows:

	Round 1	Round 2	Round 3
Schedule 1	A-B	A-C	A-D
	C-D	B-D	B-C
Schedule 2	A-B	A-D	A-C
	C-D	B-C	B-D
Schedule 3	A-C	A-B	A-D
	B-D	C-D	B-C
Schedule 4	A-C	A-D	A-B
	B-D	B-C	C-D
Schedule 5	A-D	A-B	A-C
	B-C	C-D	B-D
Schedule 6	A-D	A-C	A-B
	B-C	B-D	C-D

There are six possible schedules, and Schedules 1 and 3 are such that the A-D match takes place in the last round. Out of the six outcomes, two are such that the event of interest occurs; therefore, its probability is 2/6 = 1/3.

An interesting feature of probability distributions is that they are equally applicable whether or not the outcomes of the experiment are numbers. Situations in which the observations are not numbers occur very frequently in the social sciences. Examples include interviewing people about their preference as to candidates for presidency, observing what goods are purchased by the customers of a retail store, or which schedule of games is selected by random drawing. In such cases, many of the commonly used statistics cannot be applied. The probabilities associated with the outcomes describe the experiment entirely. Summary information can be given by telling whether the categories are approximately equally probable or whether a few of them have higher probabilities than others. The minimal and maximal probabilities occurring can also be given. Categories with maximum probabilities are called *modal categories* or *modes*.

When the outcomes of the experiment are numbers, such as the number of school years the respondent has completed or the number of terms an elected official has served, we say that the value of a variable is observed. In a stochastic model, when the different values occur with given probabilities, the variable is called a *random variable*. In the discrete case, a random variable consists of its possible values and their respective probabilities. For example, if 20% of the population of interest completed 8 years of education, 40% completed 12 years of education, 35% completed 15 years, and 5% completed 17 years, then one has a random variable with the possible values of 8, 12, 15, and 17, with respective probabilities 0.2, 0.4, 0.35, and 0.05. The probabilities form a probability distribution. The probabilities of events associated with the experiment (e.g., having 15 years of schooling or more) can be determined using the general rules (the probability of having had 15 or more years of education is 0.4, in the example).

Random variables give a complete description of the experiment with outcomes and probabilities. Various measures are available to summarize important aspects of the typical observations. The most important of these is the *expected value* of the random variable. This quantity, contrary to its name, is not the value one expects to see when the experiment is performed or the random variable is observed. Rather, it is the average of all possible values with the probabilities of these values used as weights. In the above population, the expected value of the number of years completed is

$$8 \cdot 0.2 + 12 \cdot 0.4 + 15 \cdot 0.35 + 17 \cdot 0.05 = 12.5.$$

The expected value is also not the value one expects to see the most frequently (that is the mode). It is not necessarily a value that may be observed at all. The expected value, 12.5, cannot be observed in the example. A formula for the expected value can be developed as follows. Let X be a random variable, with values $X_1, X_2, \ldots, X_k$ and probabilities $P_1, P_2, \ldots, P_k$. Then the expected value of X is

$$E(X) = P_1 X_1 + P_2 X_2 + \cdots + P_k X_k.$$

The expected value, as a weighted average, has an important "middle value" property that makes it the most important *parameter of location* or of *central tendency*. Clearly, some of the values of X are smaller than $E(X)$ and some of its values are greater. In fact, the expected value—a weighted average—cannot be smaller than all values of X, and similarly, it cannot be greater than all values. For a value of X, say X_j, let us call the difference $X_j - E(X)$ the deviation of X_j (from $E(X)$). Then, the weighted sum of positive deviations (for values greater than the expected value) is equal to the weighted sum of negative deviations (for values smaller than the expected value). In this sense, the values of a random variable deviate around its expected value. The positive and negative deviation (stemming from values above and below the expected value) cancel out. The $X_j - E(X)$ deviations with the respective probability of X_j may be considered a random variable. This may be denoted by $X - E(X)$. It is a transform of X. Its values are obtained by subtracting $E(X)$ from the values of X, and the probabilities associated with these values are the same as the probabilities of the values of X. Its expected value is the sum of the weighted sums considered above. Therefore, the expected value of $X - E(X)$ is zero.

A further important summary of the typical behavior of the random variable measures how large the deviations are around the expected value. Although the expected value of these deviations, $E(X - E(X))$, may appear to be a reasonable quantity to measure the typical size of deviations, it cannot be used because it is always zero. If one wants to prevent the positive and negative deviations from canceling out, one may take the expected value of the absolute values or of the squares of the deviations from the expected value. The first quantity obtained is called the *mean absolute deviation*, and the second one is called the *variance* of the random variable and is denoted as $V(X)$. That is,

$$V(X) = E(X - E(X))^2.$$

Note that $(X - E(X))^2$ is also a transform of X. Often, the square root of the variance, the so-called *standard deviation*, is used as the value of the typical deviation from the expected value.

The expected value and the variance have a number of important properties that can be readily derived from their definitions. If X and Y are two random variables, then $X + Y$, their sum, is also a random variable. Then,

$$E(X + Y) = E(X) + E(Y).$$

A further important transformation is to multiply every value of a random variable by a constant. Then,

$$E(cX) = cE(X).$$

For variances, one obtains

$$V(cX) = c^2 V(X).$$

If a constant is added to a random variable, the expected value will be shifted by c but the variance remains unchanged:

$$E(X + c) = E(X) + c$$

$$V(X + c) = V(X).$$

If X and Y are independent, then

$$V(X + Y) = V(X) + V(Y).$$

The *independence* of two random variables is defined as independence for as many pairs of events as the product of the respective numbers of different values of the random variables. The event that X is equal to one of its values and the event that Y is equal to one of its values should be independent for any choice of the values of X and Y. Notice that for the additivity of expected values, no independence assumption was needed. Also, the foregoing rule implies that additivity does not hold true for standard deviations.

4.2 The Binomial Distribution

The binomial is one of the most frequently occurring probability distributions in the applications of statistics in the social sciences. It often occurs as a *sampling distribution*, that is, one that describes the distribution of different possible samples in a certain situation. In such cases, the population is characterized by a certain property: Some in the population possess it, and some do not. For example, some people want to vote for a candidate for president, the others do not; or some of the applicants are admitted to graduate school, the others are not. In these examples, the populations of interest are those eligible to vote and those applying for admission to graduate school, respectively. In many real-life situations, observation of all members of the population is not feasible, so surveys are conducted to collect information. For example, an opinion poll may be used to predict the results of an election. The surveys are based on interviewing only a part of the population—those selected into the sample—and the results are generalized to the entire population. The actual survey results usually differ from each other (and also from the result that would be obtained if the entire population was interviewed), depending on who actually gave responses. These differences, due to sampling, are described in the sampling distribution. Let p denote the fraction of those in the population who possess the characteristic of interest. Thus, p is also the probability of observing a person with that characteristic, if people are selected with equal probability for observation, as, for example, in simple random sampling. If a sample of size n is considered, the number of those with the characteristic of interest may be 0, 1, 2, . . . , n. For example, if 2,000 people are interviewed about their preferred presidential candidate, the number of those naming a particular candidate may be anywhere between 0 and 2,000. But these results are not equally likely. As will be seen, results with frequencies such that the relative frequency is close to the true proportion p are more likely to occur than are relative frequencies far from p. This is exactly the fact underlying the standard method of estimation in such situations: The relative frequency of those preferring a candidate can be used to estimate the fraction of the population that would vote for this candidate.

The binomial distribution gives the probability of observing any frequency between 0 and n, assuming the true proportion is p. Let X be the random variable whose value is the frequency of the outcome of interest. Then, the probability that $X = k$, when $k = 0, 1, 2, . . . , n$, is

$$P(X = k) = Cp^k(1 - p)^{(n-k)},$$

where C is a quantity that does not depend on p, only on n and k. Note that the formula relies heavily on the fact that the n observations are selected independently from each other, and everyone in the population has the same chance of being selected into the sample. The term p^k is related to the probability of selecting k persons (independently of each other) with the characteristic, that is, observing k events of probability p, and the term $(1 - p)^{(n-k)}$ is related to the probability of selecting $n - k$ persons (independently of each other) without the characteristic, that is, observing $n - k$ events of probability $1 - p$. But these observations may be obtained in several different ways, and that is taken into account by the multiplier C. If one denotes for every integer m the product of all the integers from 1 to m by m! (read: m factorial), then $C = n!/((n - k)!k!)$. Note that, by definition, $0! = 1$. The values of n and p are said to be the parameters of the binomial distribution.

To justify the formula, consider a population of four individuals, A, B, C, and D, and suppose that A, B, and C possess the property of interest, and D does not. Therefore, $p = 3/4$. The possible samples of size $n = 2$, with the number of those possessing the property, are as follows:

AA: 2, AB: 2, AC: 2, AD: 1,

BA: 2, BB: 2, BC: 2, BD: 1,

CA: 2, CB: 2. CC: 2, CD: 1,

DA: 1, DB: 1, DC: 1, DD: 0.

There are 16 samples of size 2 (for the time being, disregard the fact that many of us would not consider AA, BB, CC, or DD a sample at all, and would not consider AB and BA, etc., as different samples). Out of these, there is one (DD) with 0, six with 1, and nine with 2 observations of those possessing the characteristic. The probabilities are therefore

$$P(X = 0) = 1/16, P(X = 1) = 6/16, P(X = 2) = 9/16.$$

The probabilities from the formula are computed as follows:

$$P(X = 0) = 2!/((2!)(0!))(3/4)^0(1/4)^2 = 1/16,$$

$$P(X = 1) = 2!/((1!)(1!))(3/4)^1(1/4)^1 = 6/16,$$

$$P(X = 2) = 2!/((0!)(2!))(3/4)^2(1/4)^0 = 9/16.$$

The formula supplies the correct probability values, if subsets containing the same individual twice are also taken into account. In practice, every social scientist would refuse to interview the same person twice, and such subsets are not considered to be samples. In our small example, 4 of the 16 samples (AA, BB, CC, DD) had that property. For large populations, the probability of selecting the same person repeatedly becomes very small, and such subsets may be omitted without affecting the validity of the formula given above. Out of the remaining samples, AB and BA, and so on, were counted separately, but because each real sample consisting of two different individuals occurs twice (in two different orders of the observations), distinguishing between the pairs that differ only in order does not lead to results different from those obtained by considering AB and BA, and so on, as the same sample.

In general, it may be checked by computing the probabilities associated with the binomial distribution that the most likely values of frequency k are near the value t, for which $t/n = p$. This t is not necessarily an integer, and therefore, no k may be equal to it. As one moves the value of k away from $t = np$, the probabilities associated with it decrease. This also implies that when observing a binomial distribution, relative frequencies, and with them estimates of the probability p, typically will be close to the true value. More precisely, the worse an estimated value, the less likely it is to be obtained. The probabilities of a binomial distribution with parameters 20 and 0.5 are

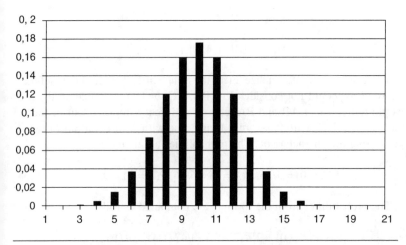

Figure 4.1   The Binomial Distribution With Parameters 20 and 0.5

shown in Figure 4.1. The expected value is 10 (see below), and that is also the value with the largest probability. The further away a value is from 10, the smaller is its probability. The values 0, 1, 2, 3, 4, 5, 15, 16, 17, 18, 19, and 20 have a total probability less than 0.05. In other words, one can expect to observe a value deviating from the expected value by 5 or more, only about once out of 20 repetitions of the experiment (here, the experiment involves 20 observations).

The expected value and variance of a binomial distribution may be determined surprisingly easily. The case of one observation only can be computed directly.

In this case, X may have either one of two values, 1 or 0, depending on whether the observation does or does not possess the property of interest. The probability that $X = 1$ is p, and the probability that $X = 0$ is $1 - p$. These probabilities also follow from the general formula for the binomial distribution, with the understanding that $0! = 1$. Therefore, the expected value of X in the case of $n = 1$ is $1p + 0(1 - p) = p$. For values of n other than 1, one should notice that counting the frequency (0, 1, 2, . . . , n) of a certain outcome out of n repetitions of the experiment is the same as counting the frequency (0 or 1) in the case of every experiment (i.e., one observation) and then adding these frequencies. Therefore, a binomial random variable with parameters n and p is the sum of n binomial random variables with parameters 1 and p. Applying the rule for the sum of expected values, one obtains that the expected value of a binomial random variable with parameters n and p is equal to n times the expected value of a binomial random variable with parameters 1 and p, that is, np.

In the example with population of size 4 and sample size 2 above, the binomial variable had three values—0, 1, and 2—with probabilities 1/16, 6/16, and 9/16, respectively. By computing the expected value based on its definition, one obtains that it is equal to 0 times 1/16 plus 1 times 6/16 plus 2 times 9/16, that is, 24/16 = 3/2. The formula np in this case gives 2 times 3/4, which is the same. If the disturbing AA, BB, CC, and DD samples are removed, one is left with 12 samples, out of which 6 have frequency 1 and 6 have frequency 2, yielding the same expected value again.

To obtain the variance of a binomial random variable, the previous argument can be repeated. The variance, with parameters 1 and p, is $(1-p)^2 p + (0-p)^2(1-p)$, where 1 and 0 are the possible values, p and $1-p$ are their respective probabilities, and p is also the expected value. After some simplification, one obtains that the variance is $p(1-p)$. Taking into account that the repetitions of the experiment are independent of each other, the summation rule for the variance can be applied, and the variance of the binomial random variable is $np(1-p)$.

The binomial distribution occurs frequently in practice. Opinion polls, for example, often report relative frequencies (in the form of percentages) as their major findings. Because the binomial distribution describes the distribution of the frequency of an event, and the relative frequency is a simple transform of it, the distribution of the relative frequency can be obtained. The possible values of the relative frequency are 0, 1/n, 2/n, . . . , 1. The probabilities associated with these values are exactly the probabilities in the binomial distribution associated with 0, 1, 2, . . . , n. The relative frequency, as a random variable, is constant (1/n) times the frequency, as a random variable. Therefore, the expected value of the relative frequency is equal to (1/n) times the expected value of the frequency. Thus, the expected value of the relative frequency of an event of probability p is (1/n)np = p. This result is important not only because of its several applications, but also because it shows how probability theory incorporates the fundamental assumption we used to introduce the concept of probability. It was assumed that the probability of an event is a number that governs its relative frequency in the sense that the relative frequency, when computed for long sequences of repetitions, approximates it. The fact that the expected value of the relative frequency is the probability means that the "middle value" of the relative frequencies is the probability. This is sometimes formulated by saying that relative frequencies deviate around the probability.

How small these deviations become for long sequences of repetitions (i.e., for large samples) is a question that, in addition to being relevant from a theoretical point of view, is also very important in practice: How far may the relative frequency (e.g., the fraction of people intending to vote for a certain candidate) in a sample be from the true value in the population? To answer this question, one uses the so-called normal approximation to the binomial distribution, to be discussed later in this chapter. It is a fine example of how assuming infinitely many observations may be helpful in obtaining important results for the finite case.

Several of the questions routinely asked in a questionnaire can have more than two responses. Binomial random variables can handle only data arising from observations with two outcomes (yes or no, male or female, does possess the property or does not). When the experiment has more than two outcomes, a generalization of the binomial distribution, the so-called polynomial distribution, is used. Here, one counts the frequency of every possible outcome. For example, if the experiment has three outcomes and one makes five observations, the following results are possible for the frequencies:

5, 0 ,0	4, 1, 0	4, 0, 1	3, 2, 0	3, 1, 1	3, 0, 2	2, 3, 0
2, 2, 1	2, 1, 2	2, 0, 3	1, 4, 0	1, 3, 1	1, 2, 2	1, 1, 3
1, 0, 4	0, 5, 0	0, 4, 1	0, 3, 2	0, 2, 3	0, 1, 4	0, 0, 5

Every possible sample (based on a sample size of 5) is one item in the list. In the case of the binomial distribution, a similar list would contain pairs of non-negative integers such that the sum of every pair is n. These, of course, could be identified with the numbers 0, 1, 2, . . . , n, because the other number is implied to be n, n − 1, n − 2, . . . , 0. In the case of a polynomial distribution with d different outcomes, the list contains d-tuples, such that the d non-negative integers sum to the sample size (5 in the example).

One can also define random variables that take on these d-tuples as values. Such a variable is called *multidimensional* or *vector valued*. The notions of expected value and variance can be generalized to this more general case. For example, if the i-th outcome has probability p_i, then the expected value of the number of times this outcome is observed out of n repetitions of the experiment (i.e., in a sample of size n) is np_i. The variance of the number of times the i-th outcome occurs is $np_i(1 - p_i)$.

In such cases, it is also important to know how the frequencies of the different outcomes are related to each other. If there are more than two outcomes, the frequency of one of them does not entirely determine the frequency of the others. Yet there is some relationship between the frequencies of the different outcomes. It is clear that it may be the case that all the frequencies are equal to their respective expected values, because the sum of the expected values is n. On the other hand, if one frequency happens to be larger than its expected value, then the others will tend to be smaller than their respective expected values, because the sum of all frequencies is constant. This effect is more marked if the frequency that happens to be large has a relatively big expected value, and its effect is stronger on frequencies that have relatively large expected values. For example, suppose there are three candidates for president of the United States: A, B, and C, and 50%, 45%, and 5% of the voters support them. In a sample of 1,000 people, if 60 people (20% more than expected) say that they would vote for C, this has a weak effect on the frequencies of A and B. Although in total, they cannot have 950 people mentioning them, as the expected values would suggest, only 940, their frequencies can get fairly close to their expected values. If 600 people (20% more than expected) say they would vote for A, then B and C together will fall short of their expected value by quite a large amount (100, combined). But the effect on C is smaller than on B, because it may be the case that C has as many voters in the sample as expected (i.e., 50), but B will certainly have fewer than its expected value (i.e., 450). The frequencies of A, B, and C are called the *components* of the multidimensional random variable and are random variables themselves. On the other hand, the original random variable is said to have the *joint distribution* of its components.

A common measure of how strongly random variables influence each other is their *covariance*. The covariance is the expected value of a transformed random variable. If the two random variables are X and Y (note that they need to have a joint distribution to have a covariance, that is, they have to be the components of a higher dimensional random variable), then their covariance is

$$\mathrm{Cov}(X, Y) = \mathrm{E}((X - \mathrm{E}(X))(Y - \mathrm{E}(Y))).$$

The concept of covariance is best understood by considering the possible values of the transform $(X - \mathrm{E}(X))(Y - \mathrm{E}(Y))$. The behavior of $(X - \mathrm{E}(X))(Y - \mathrm{E}(Y))$ is illustrated in Figure 4.2. This random variable is positive if both $X - \mathrm{E}(X)$ and $Y - \mathrm{E}(Y)$ are positive, or if both are negative. In the first case, both X and Y are greater than their respective expected values (Quadrant II in Figure 4.2), and in the second case, they are both smaller than their respective expected values (Quadrant IV in Figure 4.2). These are situations when they deviate from their respective expected values in the same direction. The transform will be negative if the two variables deviate in opposite directions from their respective expected values. These situations occur in Quadrants I (X is relatively small and Y is relatively large) and III (X is relatively large and Y is relatively small). Therefore, the covariance of two random variables will be greater (large positive values) if they tend to deviate from their respective expected values parallel to each other, and the covariance will be small (large negative values) if they

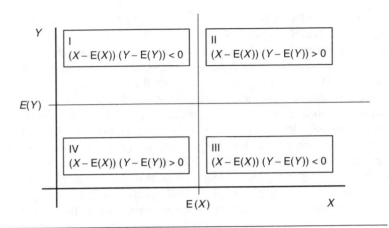

Figure 4.2   The Sign of the $(X - E(X))(Y - E(Y))$ Product

tend to deviate in opposite directions. As the foregoing argument suggests, the covariance between two components of a polynomial random variable is negative. Noting that $cov(X, X) = var(X)$ may also help in understanding the idea of covariance.

If two variables are independent, their covariance is zero. Independence implies that the deviations of X around its expected value are not related to the deviations of Y around its own expected value. Therefore, the product $(X - E(X))(Y - E(Y))$ does not have a tendency to take on positive values (which would be the case if X and Y tended to deviate in the same direction), nor does it have a tendency to take on negative values (which would be the case if X and Y tended to deviate in opposite directions), and therefore, its expected value is zero.

The interpretation of the covariance and the comparison of covariance values of different pairs of variables are difficult because its values are not scaled, that is, it is difficult to tell what is a strong covariance and what is a weak covariance. A standardized version of covariance is called *correlation*. This is obtained by dividing the covariance by the product of the standard deviations of the two variables:

$$cor(X, Y) = cov(X, Y)/(d(X)d(Y)),$$

where $d(X)$ is the standard deviation of X and $d(Y)$ is the standard deviation of Y. The correlation (or correlation coefficient) is always between -1 and 1. If the two variables are independent, then they are also uncorrelated, that is, their correlation is zero. An interesting property of the correlation coefficient is that its value does not change if the variables are transformed linearly. A linear transformation means multiplying the variable by a constant and adding a constant to it (for all its values). If a, b, c, and d are constants, then

$$\text{cor}(aX + b, \, cY + d) = \text{cor}(X, Y).$$

4.3 The Continuous Case

One can also define random variables in connection with experiments with infinitely many outcomes. The most important case is when it is assumed that all real numbers (or all real numbers in an interval) are possible outcomes of the experiment. In such cases, as discussed in the previous chapter, a density function can be used to describe the behavior of the random variable. Such a random variable is called *continuous.*

A continuous random variable assumes all its values with probability zero. It is the likelihood that may be different for the possible values. Some values are more likely to occur than others. Probability is associated with intervals and half lines and other sets derived from these (see Figure 3.5). If an interval contains another one, the former cannot have a smaller probability than the latter. On the other hand, intervals of the same length, depending on their locations on the number line, may have different probabilities. The probabilities can be read off from the density function. The probability of (having an observation in) an interval is equal to the area under the density function above the interval. Generally, higher values of the density function imply more frequent observations (see Figure 3.6).

As the simplest example of a continuous random variable, we first consider a continuous version of the uniform distribution. In this case, the possible values are that of an interval. But the continuous distribution is not defined in this case by saying that all values have the same probability, because this is not informative. Rather, it is defined by saying that all possible values have the same likelihood, or that the density function is constant over the interval. Because observations outside this interval are not supposed to occur, the density function is zero outside this interval. A practical example of when such a random variable may occur is when job satisfaction is measured by printing a horizontal line in the questionnaire, with the endpoints marked as 0 and 100%, and asking the respondents to mark the position that best represents their feelings toward their jobs. In theory, because no point can be excluded as a potential observation, and, theoretically, the position of the marks made by the respondents can be measured with arbitrary precision, one may assume that all values on the interval from 0 to 100 may be observed. The (quite unrealistic) assumption that all responses are equally likely leads to a density as shown in Figure 4.3.

48

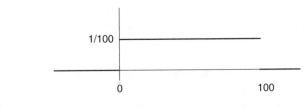

Figure 4.3   A Uniform Density Function

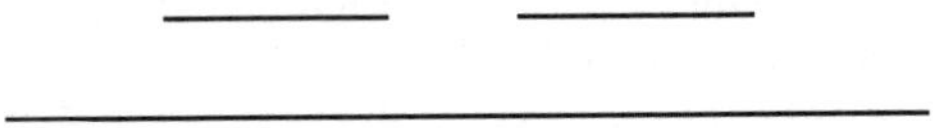

Figure 4.4   Uniform Densities With Different Locations

The function is constant over the interval (0, 100) and is also constant outside of it. Outside of the interval (i.e., for negative values and values above 100), the density is zero. The value of the density function over the (0, 100) interval is determined by the requirement that the total area under the density function is equal to one. The density over (0, 100) is equal to 1/100. The probability of having an observation in any subinterval of (0, 100) is proportional to the length of this subinterval and does not depend on the position of the interval. This is why this distribution is called uniform. For example, the probability of having an observation between 50 and 60 is (60 − 50) (1/100) = 0.1, and this is the probability of any interval of length 10.

A random variable with a uniform distribution can also be characterized by its expected value and by the amount of variation around it. For example, Figure 4.4 illustrates the density functions of two uniform distributions with different locations. The observations from the density to the right are always larger than the observations from the density to the left. In the case of two overlapping densities (e.g., one in the interval (10, 20) and another one in the interval (15, 25)), one could say that the observations from the second one are generally, or on average, larger than the observations from the first one. A precise formulation of the concept of the expected value requires the definition of a general form of weighted average. In the case of a uniform distribution, the values to be averaged, the possible values, are those in the interval where the density is not zero, and the weights are the appropriate values of the density function. But because these values are all equal, symmetry implies that the expected value is the average of the endpoints of the interval. If the job satisfaction values are uniformly distributed over the interval (0, 100), then their expected value is 50.

The expected value can also be obtained by approximating the continuous uniform variable with a discrete one. If one considers the continuous variable that is not zero over the interval (0, 100), then a discrete approximation is obtained by dividing the interval into, say, 100 intervals of length 1. These intervals are (0, 1], (1, 2], (2, 3], . . . , (98, 99], (99, 100). The probability of each of these intervals is 1/100. The discrete approximation is obtained by choosing an arbitrary value in every small interval, such as the midpoint, and associating the probability of the small interval with the selected value. The midpoints of the small intervals are 0.5, 1.5, 2.5, . . . , 99.5. This defines a discrete random variable with 100 possible values and uniform distribution, because each value has the same probability, namely 1/100. This discrete variable is an approximation of the original continuous variable, and the approximation can be made better by dividing the interval (0, 100) not into 100 but into 1,000, 10,000, or 100,000 smaller intervals.

The expected value of the discrete variable can be easily determined. When the possible values are 0.5, 1.5, 2.5, . . . , 99.5, the expected value is simply their average (because they are equally likely), namely 50. It is easy to see that the expected values of other possible approximating discrete variables obtained by using 1,000, 10,000, or 100,000 intervals like the 100 intervals that are used above, are equal to 50. As the discrete variables approximate the continuous variable, their expected values should also approximate its expected value, and, therefore, the expected value[2] of the uniform distribution over the interval (0, 100) is, in fact, 50, or the midpoint of the interval.

Two uniform densities with different locations were illustrated in Figure 4.4. The density functions have the same shapes, and the expected values are the respective midpoints of the intervals.

The concept of variance is also meaningful for continuous variables. It is defined as the expected value of a transformed variable, namely, the square of the deviation from the expected value. If X is a continuous uniform random variable in the interval (a, b), then its expected value is $E(X) = (a + b)/2$. The variance is $V(X) = E((X - E(X)^2) = (b - a)^2/12$. It is intuitively clear that a variable with a uniform distribution over a larger interval has more variation around the expected value than a variable having a uniform distribution over a shorter interval. Two uniform densities with the same mean but different variances are shown in Figure 4.5.

The distribution over the longer (a, b) interval has a lower density value than the distribution over the shorter (c, d) interval, so that the area under either function is equal to 1. Because the two intervals have the same midpoint, the two distributions have the same expected value. The distribution over the longer interval has a larger deviation around its expected value than the distribution over the shorter interval. This is also implied by the formula, because b – a is greater than d – c in the present case.

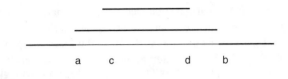

a   c   d   b

Figure 4.5   Uniform Densities With Different Variances

The concepts of expected value and variance can be defined in the case of continuous random variables with other density functions as well. The expected value remains a generalization of the weighted average: It is a midpoint that takes into account not only the possible values but also their different likelihoods. If, however, the density function is symmetric around a certain point, then the expected value will be that point. One way to derive the expected value in the continuous case is by using discrete approximations, as illustrated earlier for the uniform distribution. One such approximation is obtained by covering the number line by a (finite) number of adjacent intervals and two half lines (one containing all numbers smaller than the lower endpoint of the first interval and one containing all numbers larger than the upper endpoint of the last interval). This is illustrated in Figure 4.6, where $I_2, \ldots, I_{10}$ are adjacent intervals and I_1 and I_{11} are half lines, so that they jointly cover the entire line. For simplicity, all will be referred to as intervals in what follows. It is not important whether or not the intervals are of equal length. In every interval, select a value, say, a_i, within the i-th interval. It does not have to be the midpoint of the interval. The value a_3 is shown in Figure 4.6. Furthermore, let p_i denote the probability of the i-th interval. The value of p_4 is shown as a shaded area.

Then, the sum of $a_i p_i$ for all intervals is an approximation of the expected value. Here, the continuous random variable is approximated by a discrete one, having the values a_i with respective probabilities p_i. There are, of course, several approximations of this type available, depending on the choice of the intervals and the values from the intervals. One can also define sequences of approximations, such that within one sequence, the intervals become shorter and shorter (more precisely, their maximum length converges to zero) and the combined length of the intervals without the half lines becomes longer and longer (more precisely, it converges to that of the entire line). For all such approximating sequences, one has a sequence of expected values. If all these sequences converge to the same value, then we say that the expected value of the continuous random variable exists and is equal to the common limit. Although this may appear to be quite a complex definition, it is good to know that for continuous

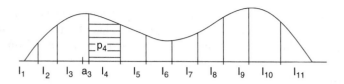

Figure 4.6   Finite Approximation of the Expected Value

density functions that may occur in statistical applications in the social sciences, the expected value always exists and can be found by considering one approximating sequence only.

To illustrate how the above procedure works, the expected value of the uniform distribution over the interval (0, 100) will now be approximated by a sequence different from the one used earlier. First, choose the intervals (0, 1], (1, 2], . . . , (98, 99], (99, 100), and the right-hand side endpoint of each of them: 1, 2, . . . , 100. The probability associated with each of these intervals is 1/100. The half lines outside the interval (0, 100) need not be considered, because the probabilities associated with them and with their subsets are zero. Therefore, the first approximating sum is 1 • 1/100 + 2 • 1/100 + · · · + 100 • 1/100. Because the sum (1 + 2 + · · · + 100) is equal to 5,050, the first approximation is 5,050/100 = 50.5. Next, divide each interval into 10 equal parts. One has 1,000 intervals, each with probability 1/1000. Again, choose as representative values the endpoints on the right-hand sides: 0.1, 0.2, . . . , 99.9, 100. Then, the approximating sum is the sum of these values divided by 1,000. This gives 50,050/1,000 = 50.05. In the next step, the intervals are again divided into ten equal parts and the approximating sum is 50.005. One obtains an approximating sequence by continuing this procedure. This sequence converges to 50, and this is the expected value of the uniform distribution on the interval (0, 100).

The properties of expected value, discussed in detail for discrete variables, remain true. This includes the properties of transforms. Most importantly, the expected value of the deviations of a variable from its own expected value is zero; the expected value of a sum is the sum of the expected values; and if a variable is multiplied by a constant, then the expected value is also multiplied by the same constant. Transformations of a random variable also affect its density function. For example, if a constant c is added to a random variable, its density function is shifted by –c. The density of $X + c$ at the value a is equal to the density of X at $a - c$, because $X = a - c$ if $X + c = a$. Similarly, multiplying a random variable by a constant leads to a rescaling of the density function.

Variance and standard deviation for continuous random variables are also defined by a straightforward generalization of the definitions in the discrete case. The variance is the expected value of the squared deviations from the expected value. The variance is the expected value of a transform of the original variable. The relevant transformation is subtracting, from each value of the random variable, the expected value and then taking the square of the difference. This yields a continuous random variable, the expected value of which is the variance of the original random variable. Note that if the difference is not squared, the expected value is zero. The standard deviation is the square root of the variance. The value of the standard deviation can be interpreted as the typical value of the deviation of the random variable from its expected value.

Covariance and correlation can also be defined in the continuous case. One only has to realize that, if the two variables have a joint distribution, the covariance is the expected value of a transform of the two variables. The properties and interpretations of covariance and of correlation remain true, because these properties carry over for approximating sequences.

4.4 The Normal Distribution

This section discusses the most important continuous distribution in the theory and applications of statistics. There are a number of practical and conceptual reasons for this importance. The normal distribution, just like any other continuous distribution, is an approximation to reality, but it is an approximation that can be applied very frequently.

A typical situation in which the normal distribution is a good approximation of reality is the distribution of errors in a physical measurement, such as length or weight. Measuring the same object using the same instrument repeatedly usually leads to different results and produces histograms similar to the density of a normal distribution. Measurement results close to the true value are more likely to occur than results far from the true value: Small errors are more likely than large ones. Also, the distribution of the measurement results is symmetric around the true value: Positive errors are just as likely to occur as negative errors. In practice, lack of precision in reading the results (compared to the differences in the measurements) often hides the fact that the results are, in reality, different from each other. The typical magnitude of the differences among measurement results for the same object (to be modeled in theory by standard deviation) is an indicator of the precision of the measuring instrument. Electronic measuring devices often make a number of measurements automatically and report their average value, to make up for possible fluctuations among the results of individual measurements.

Similar phenomena can be observed in the applications of statistics in the social sciences. For example, an opinion poll may be considered a measuring instrument of, say, the level of support for proposed new legislation among the population. If the poll is conducted repeatedly (more precisely, polls applying the same methodology are conducted in parallel to each other), then the results will be different. Here, the reason for different results is sampling, that is, the different polls are based on different samples and the respondents will give, on average, slightly different answers. In this case, the distribution of the different results can be well approximated by a normal distribution. This gives us very useful tools for estimating the true value for the entire population.

A further interesting property of the normal distribution is that if one considers several random variables that are independent from each other and then their average, the distribution of the average[3] can be approximated by a normal distribution. This is true under very mild conditions that almost always hold true for observations in the social sciences. The original variables, of which the average is taken, need not even be continuous. The larger the number of variables, the better a normal distribution approximates the distribution of their average. If the original variables are "close" to being normal, the approximation is better, but by increasing the number of variables that are averaged, the approximation can be made arbitrarily precise, whatever the distribution of the original variables. This (mathematical) fact is often referred to as the central limit theorem.

The central limit theorem is the mathematical reason for believing that the deviation in the results of the different polls from the true value (the one that could be obtained by a census) is similar to the normal distribution. If the fraction of those who support the proposed legislation is p, then because the poll selects respondents from the population with equal probabilities and independently from each other, the probability that a respondent expresses support is p, and the total number of respondents in the sample supporting the new law has a binomial distribution. When the expected value of the binomial distribution was determined, we already used the 0–1 indicator variables that can be associated with each respondent. The binomial variable X (the frequency) is the sum of these. As an estimator of the true fraction p, one uses the relative frequency X/n, where n is the sample size. This relative frequency is the average of the indicator variables, because there are n such variables and their sum is X. The central limit theorem applies, and for large samples, the relative frequency—and therefore, the estimate of p from the sample—deviates around its expected value similarly to a normal distribution. This means that the properties of the normal distribution may be used to describe the behavior of simple estimators from surveys. The larger the sample size, the better the approximation. The expected value of the estimator X/n is the expected value of X divided by n, that is, $np/n = p$, the true value.

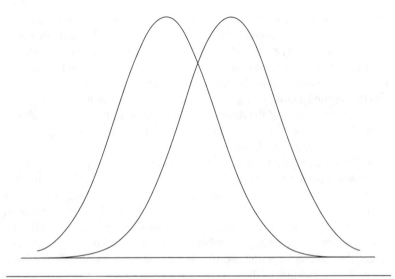

Figure 4.7   Normal Densities With Different Locations

A further situation in which normality is relevant arises from the fact that the central limit theorem justifies assuming that the observations will be distributed with a good approximation to normal, if the value reported by the respondents is the average of several independent factors. For example, if one believes that overall job satisfaction is the result of several aspects that influence it independently of each other, then the reported job satisfaction is close to being normally distributed. In psychology, intelligence is usually considered to be an overall measure of several components (such as verbal intelligence, spatial intelligence, etc.) that occur independently of each other, and, therefore, is assumed to have a normal distribution (see Lord, 1968).

The normal distribution is not one probability distribution but rather a family of probability distributions. A normal distribution (one from the family of normal distributions) is entirely characterized by its expected value and variance. The expected value can be any number, and the variance can be any positive number. In fact, for arbitrarily selected expected value and (positive) variance, there exists a normal distribution. The distributions in the normal family have densities of a special shape, often said to be the shape of a bell. As is true in the general case, the expected value determines location, and (the square root of) the variance determines the typical size of deviation around the expected value. Figure 4.7 illustrates two normal densities with the same variance but different locations. The

Figure 4.8   Normal Densities With Different Variances

two densities are of the same shape. The normal density is symmetric, and the point of symmetry is the expected value. A difference in the expected value means a shift between the two densities.

Figure 4.8 illustrates two normal densities with the same location but different variances. The two densities are centered around the same value (the common expected value), but one shows a larger amount of deviation around it. Values further away from the expected value, in the case of this density, have greater likelihoods than with the other density.

Within the family of normal distributions, the one with an expected value equal to 0 and variance equal to 1 (and, therefore, also a standard deviation equal to 1), is called the *standard normal distribution*. Any random variable having a normal distribution can be transformed into a standard normal variable. The procedure is called *standardization*. Moreover, the transformation is very simple: One has to subtract the expected value and divide by the standard deviation. If Y is a normal random variable having expected value a and variance b^2, then $(Y - a)/b$ is a random variable with standard normal distribution. The fact that $(Y - a)/b$ has zero expected value and unit standard deviation follows from our previous results. Because $E(Y) = a$, $E(Y - a) = 0$. Subtracting a constant does not change the variance, therefore, the variance of $Y - a$ is equal to b^2, and thus, the variance of $(Y - a)/b$, that is, the variance of $Y - a$ divided by b^2, is $b^2/b^2 = 1$. A variable with zero expected value and unit variance is called standard. The fact that the standard form of a normal variable remains normal is an important characteristic of the family of normal distributions. This relationship can be used to determine probabilities associated with normally distributed variables, if only the density function of a standard normal variable is known. If X is a standard normal variable, then t ≤ Y ≤ u if and only if (t – a)/b ≤ X ≤ (t – u)/b. Therefore, the probability that Y is in the interval (t, u) is the same as the probability that the standard normal variable, X, is in the interval ((t – a)/b, (t – u)/b). Such probabilities can be determined from Table 4.1.

For example, if Y has expected value 2 and variance 2.25, then the probability that it is in the interval (2, 3.5) is the same as that the standard normal is in the interval ((2 – 2)/1.5, (3.5 – 2)/1.5), that is, in the interval (0, 1). (Here, 1.5 is the standard deviation of Y.) That probability can be determined from Table 4.1 as follows. X is between 0 and 1 if it is less than 1 but not less than zero. Therefore, to obtain the probability that it is between 0 and 1, one has to take the probability that it is less than 1 and subtract from it the probability that it is less than zero. These two probabilities, from Table 4.1, are 0.84 and 0.5, respectively, and their difference is 0.34. Thus, the probability that a normal variable with expected value 2 and variance 2.25 is between 2 and 3.5 is 0.34.

The standardization procedure of a normal variable shows that common properties of all normal distributions can be formulated in terms of the expected value and the standard deviation. Table 4.1 shows that the standard normal distribution is symmetric around zero. For example, the likelihood of 1 is equal to that of –1. Consequently, positive and negative observations occur with the same probability. Because observing 0 has zero probability, both positive and negative values have probability 0.5. What can be said about a general normal variable? Its distribution is not symmetric around zero, but rather around the value that is transformed into zero when standardization is carried out. In standardization, because one subtracts the expected value (and then divides by the standard deviation), the value that transforms into zero is the expected value. Therefore, any normal density is symmetric around its expected value.

The probability that a standard normal variable deviates from zero by more than 2, that is, its observed value is less than –2 or more than 2, is the sum of the probabilities of these disjoint events. Each has a probability of 0.02228; therefore, the probability of a deviation from the expected value of more than 2 is 0.04456. For simplicity, we round[4] this value to 0.05 and say that, in the case of a standard normal distribution, the event of observing values that deviate by 2 or more from zero has a probability of 0.05 and, as the opposite event, the probability that an observation deviates from zero by less than 2 is 0.95. For general normal distributions, the amount of deviation that transforms into a deviation of 2 after standardization is a deviation equal to the amount of two standard deviations. When the expected value is subtracted from a value of the variable larger than the expected value, one obtains the deviation. The deviation is divided by the standard deviation. As a result, one obtains 2 if the actual deviation was equal to twice the standard deviation. This implies that the probability that a normal variable deviates from its expected value by less than twice its standard deviation is 0.95.

The foregoing argument suggests considering the expected value as the starting point of a scale on which to measure deviations, and the standard deviation as the unit of measuring its magnitude. Then, the relevant results can be read from Table 4.1 by using zero instead of the expected value and 1 instead of the standard deviation.

In particular, one obtains the following characteristic properties of every normal distribution:

The probability that an observation does not deviate more from the expected value than the standard deviation is about 0.67 or 2/3.

The probability that an observation does not deviate more from the expected value than twice the standard deviation is about 0.95 or 19/20.

The probability that an observation does not deviate more from the expected value than three times the standard deviation is about 0.997 or 299/300.

The above rules are particularly useful in statistics. The central limit theorem implies that the average of the observations, for large samples, is approximately normal. If one observes a variable with variance equal to, say, a^2, then because the observations are selected independently, the variance of the sum of observations is the sum of variances, na^2, if the sample size is n. When the average is computed, the sum is divided by n. In this transformation, the variance is divided by the square of this quantity, n^2. Therefore, the variance of the average is a^2/n, where a^2 is the original variance of the observations. This implies that for larger samples, the variance of the average will be smaller and can be used as a better estimate of the expected value of the original variables. For example, consider a binomial variable. Here, the goal is to estimate the true proportion p from a sample. As discussed earlier, the variance of the binomial random variable (the sum) is $np(1 - p)$, and therefore, the variance of the average (the relative frequency) is $p(1 - p)/n$. For fixed p, this quantity reduces in proportion to n. Therefore, the standard deviation decreases in proportion to the square root of the sample size.

Because the true value of p is not known, it is useful to consider an upper limit of the variance for all values of p, depending on the sample size n. Such an upper limit is obtained if p is assumed to be 0.5. The upper limits of the standard deviation (the square root of the variance) for different sample sizes are given in Table 4.2.

58

TABLE 4.1
Probabilities Associated With a Standard Normal Distribution

Value (x)	Likelihood of x	Probability of an Observation Smaller Than x	Probability of an Observation Larger Than x
− 3	0.0044	0.0014	0.9987
− 2.9	0.0060	0.0019	0.9981
− 2.8	0.0079	0.0026	0.9974
− 2.7	0.0104	0.0035	0.9965
− 2.6	0.0136	0.0047	0.9953
− 2.5	0.0175	0.0062	0.9938
− 2.4	0.0224	0.0082	0.9918
− 2.3	0.0283	0.0107	0.9893
− 2.2	0.0355	0.0139	0.9861
− 2.1	0.0440	0.0179	0.9821
− 2	0.0540	0.0228	0.9772
− 1.9	0.0656	0.0287	0.9713
− 1.8	0.0790	0.0359	0.9641
− 1.7	0.0940	0.0446	0.9554
− 1.6	0.1109	0.0548	0.9452
− 1.5	0.1295	0.0668	0.9332
− 1.4	0.1497	0.0808	0.9192
− 1.3	0.1714	0.0968	0.9032
− 1.2	0.1942	0.1151	0.8849
− 1.1	0.2179	0.1357	0.8643
− 1	0.2420	0.1587	0.8413
− 0.9	0.2661	0.1841	0.8159
− 0.8	0.2897	0.2119	0.7881
− 0.7	0.3123	0.2420	0.7580
− 0.6	0.3332	0.2743	0.7257
− 0.5	0.3521	0.3085	0.6915
− 0.4	0.3683	0.3446	0.6554
− 0.3	0.3814	0.3821	0.6179
− 0.2	0.3910	0.4207	0.5793
− 0.1	0.3970	0.4602	0.5398
0	0.3989	0.5000	0.5000
0.1	0.3970	0.5398	0.4602
0.2	0.3910	0.5793	0.4207
0.3	0.3814	0.6179	0.3821
0.4	0.3683	0.6554	0.3446
0.5	0.3521	0.6915	0.3085
0.6	0.3332	0.7257	0.2743
0.7	0.3123	0.7580	0.2420
0.8	0.2897	0.7881	0.2119
0.9	0.2661	0.8159	0.1841
1	0.2420	0.8413	0.1587

Value (x)	Likelihood of x	Probability of an Observation Smaller Than x	Probability of an Observation Larger Than x
1.1	0.2179	0.8643	0.1357
1.2	0.1942	0.8849	0.1151
1.3	0.1714	0.9032	0.0968
1.4	0.1497	0.9192	0.0808
1.5	0.1295	0.9332	0.0668
1.6	0.1109	0.9452	0.0548
1.7	0.0940	0.9554	0.0446
1.8	0.0790	0.9641	0.0359
1.9	0.0656	0.9713	0.0287
2	0.0540	0.9773	0.0228
2.1	0.0440	0.9821	0.0179
2.2	0.0355	0.9861	0.0139
2.3	0.0283	0.9893	0.0107
2.4	0.0224	0.9918	0.0082
2.5	0.0175	0.9938	0.0062
2.6	0.0136	0.9953	0.0047
2.7	0.0104	0.9965	0.0035
2.8	0.0079	0.9974	0.0026
2.9	0.0060	0.9981	0.0019
3	0.0044	0.9987	0.0014

TABLE 4.2
Upper Limits for the Standard Deviation of a Relative Frequency

Sample Size	50	100	500	1,000	1,500	2,000	2,500	3,000
Standard deviation	0.070711	0.05	0.022361	0.015811	0.01291	0.01118	0.01	0.009129

One sees that, for example, when using a sample size of 1,000, the standard error of the relative frequency is about 0.016. Combining this with the normal approximation and the results for the normal distribution, one sees that in this case, the deviation between the true fraction and the estimated fraction will not be more than 0.032, which is the value of two times the standard deviation in 95% of the applications of the procedure. In other words, only 1 out of 20 surveys can be expected to make an error in excess of 0.032, if using a sample size of 1,000. Furthermore, using the rule about deviations greater than three standard errors, only 1 out of 300 surveys is expected to have an error larger than 0.048. These results are very important in assessing the precision of survey results and in determining the necessary sample size when a certain accuracy of results is required.

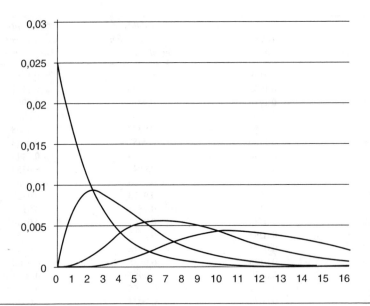

Figure 4.9   Densities of Chi-Squared Distributions With 2, 4, 8, and 12
Degrees of Freedom

4.5 The Chi-Squared Distribution

Another frequently occurring distribution in the applications of statistics in the social sciences is the chi-squared distribution. It is a good approximation of the distribution of the most frequently applied test statistics when the independence of two categorical variables or, more generally, a log-linear model (Knoke & Burke, 1980) is fitted.

The chi-squared distribution has a parameter, usually called the degree of freedom. The chi-squared distribution with, say, d degrees of freedom is defined as the distribution of a variable equal to the sum of d independent squared standard normal distributions. This implies that a variable with a chi-squared distribution cannot be negative. Therefore, the density is zero for negative values. For small and moderate values of d, the chi-squared density is far from being symmetric. Relatively large values occur with smaller likelihoods. The densities of chi-squared distributions with d = 2, 4, 8, and 12 are shown in Figure 4.9. The density is unimodal, and for larger d values, the value of the mode is larger.

For applications of the chi-squared distribution, more important than the density itself are those values with the property that observations above

TABLE 4.3
Critical Values of the Chi-Squared Distribution

Degrees of Freedom	0.01	0.05	0.10
1	6.6349	3.8415	2.7055
2	9.2104	5.9915	4.6052
3	11.3449	7.8147	6.2514
4	13.2767	9.4877	7.7794
5	15.0863	11.0705	9.2363
6	16.8119	12.5916	10.6446
7	18.4753	14.0671	12.0170
8	20.0902	15.5073	13.3616
9	21.6660	16.9190	14.6837
10	23.2093	18.3070	15.9872
12	26.2170	21.0261	18.5493
14	29.1412	23.6848	21.0641
16	31.9999	26.2962	23.5418
18	34.8052	28.8693	25.9894
20	37.5663	31.4104	28.4120
25	44.3140	37.6525	34.3816
30	50.8922	43.7730	40.2560
35	57.3420	49.8018	46.0588
40	63.6908	55.7585	51.8050
45	69.9569	61.6562	57.5053
50	76.1538	67.5048	63.1671
60	88.3794	79.0820	74.3970
70	100.4251	90.5313	85.5270
80	112.3288	101.8795	96.5782
90	124.1162	113.1452	107.5650
100	135.8069	124.3421	118.4980

them occur with specified small probabilities. In statistics, it is of particular importance to know these values (often called critical values) for probabilities 0.01, 0.05, and 0.10. These are, of course, different for every degree of freedom. Such values are given in Table 4.3 for selected degree-of-freedom values between 1 and 100.

Table 4.3 can be used as follows. If a chi-squared distribution with six degrees of freedom is of interest (e.g., independence is tested in a 3×4 table), then the variable is greater than 12.59 with probability 0.05, and it is greater than 10.64 with probability 0.1. Then, 12.59 is called the 0.05 or 5% critical value of the distribution. Alternatively, 12.59 is also called the 95th percentage point of the distribution. Here again, we rely on the fact that it has probability zero to observe exactly 12.59.

62

When critical values of chi-squared variables with degrees of freedom not listed in Table 4.3 are needed, one can interpolate, that is, choose the critical value as a value in between the critical values associated with degrees of freedom immediately below and above the current one in the table. If the critical value of a chi-squared distribution with 11 degrees of freedom is needed, one may choose a value between 23.21 and 26.22, if the relevant probability level is 0.01. This procedure gives only an approximation, but approximate values are usually sufficient in the statistical applications in which critical values are used.

5. CONCLUSIONS

This book has presented the basic concepts of probability theory by emphasizing motivation, use, and interpretation rather than formal arguments. Probability theory is important in the social sciences because it gives a theoretical background for both sampling and data analysis. The correct application of statistical methods and the interpretation of the results also require familiarity with the most important concepts and results of probability theory.

The theory outlined in this book is appropriate for the analysis of situations in which observations are selected from a large population, which is the most frequent set-up for empirical research in the social sciences. The probabilities of various events associated with the observations can then be identified with the relevant population fractions. It is a starting assumption, but also a fundamental result in the theory that, assuming appropriate sample selection methods, the relative frequency of an event in the data converges to its probability if the sample size increases. The most important properties of probability are easily derived from the properties of relative frequencies. We have obtained a formula for the likely size of the deviation between the true probability and the relative frequency in the sample that is used to estimate it. We have also seen that the likely size of this deviation decreases in proportion to the square root of the sample size. Because the observed frequencies follow a binomial distribution, the normal approximation gave us practical rules concerning the expected behavior of the deviation that is the error in the estimate of the true population fraction. These results belong to the theoretical basis of any opinion polling activity.

As a summary description of an experiment with numerical outcomes and their probabilities, the notion of a random variable was introduced, and the expected value (as a weighted average of the possible values) and the variance (as a summary measure of the amount of squared variation) were defined. The square root of the variance, the standard deviation, is the typical size of difference between the expected value and an observation.

The normal distribution, introduced here as an approximation to reality, is a continuous probability distribution and proves to be useful in several applications of statistics. Random variables with a continuous distribution are handled by their respective density functions, and important parameters such as the expected value or the variance can be defined and have interpretations similar to the discrete case. The family of normal distributions can be understood by studying the standard normal distribution, because all normally distributed random variables are simple linear transforms of a standard normal variable. Normality, in addition to implying unimodality and symmetry, also means a certain level of concentration around the expected value. Another frequently occurring continuous distribution, the chi-squared distribution, also was discussed. Its importance comes from the fact that most hypothesis-testing problems for categorical data (and in many other cases as well) lead to test statistics that are, for large samples, distributed as chi-squared.

APPENDIX A

THE CUSTOMER BEHAVIOR EXAMPLE

This example is used repeatedly in the text, and its major characteristics are summarized here.

Companies: X and Y

Product brands: A, B, C, D, E

Product sizes: regular, large

A and B are brands of X, and C, D, and E are brands of Y. All brands are available in regular size, but only Brands C, D, and E are available in large size. The existing combinations with their respective notations are as follows ("na" means that the particular combination is not available).

Company	Brand	Size	
		Regular	Large
X	A	Ar	na
X	B	Br	na
Y	C	Cr	Cl
Y	D	Dr	Dl
Y	E	Er	El

In this example, the observations (outcomes) are the combinations of goods bought. Events are collections of outcomes. For example, the event that the customer bought at least two products in large size is a combination of 96 outcomes. Or, the event that Ar is bought (and possibly other products)—(Ar)—is the combination of 128 different outcomes, depending on what combination of other products was bought in addition to buying Ar.

Some important events: The event of buying a product of Company X is

$$(X) = (Ar) + (Br),$$

and the event of buying from among the products of Y is

$$(Y) = (Cr) + (Cl) + (Dr) + (Dl) + (Er) + (El).$$

The event of buying a product in large size is

$$(1) = (Cl) + (Dl) + (El).$$

The event of buying Brand E is

$$(E) = (Er) + (El).$$

66

APPENDIX B

THE PROPERTIES OF RELATIVE
FREQUENCIES AND OF PROBABILITIES

The most important properties of relative frequencies and of probabilities are summarized here. These properties are explained in the text. For probabilities, r has to be replaced by P in the notation.

Property 1. A relative frequency (probability) is always between zero and one:

$$1 \geq r(A) \geq 0.$$

Property 2. The relative frequency (probability) of the opposite of an event is one minus the relative frequency (probability) of the original event:

$$r(A^C) = 1 - r(A).$$

Property 3. The relative frequency (probability) of the certain event is one:

$$r(S) = 1,$$

and this also implies that the relative frequency (probability) of the impossible event is zero:

$$r(0) = 0.$$

Property 4. If two events cannot occur at the same time, then the relative frequency (probability) of one of them occurring is the sum of their respective relative frequencies (probabilities): If

$$EF = 0,$$

then

$$r(E) + r(F) = r(E + F).$$

Property 5. The relative frequency (probability) of the sum of two events is equal to the sum of their relative frequencies (probabilities) minus the relative frequency (probability) of their product:

$$r(E) + r(F) = r(E + F) - r(EF).$$

NOTES

1. All real numbers cannot be ordered to form a sequence. A sketch of the proof is given here for real numbers between 0 and 1. Write all these numbers in the decimal form. One has a zero followed by a certain number of digits after the decimal point for every number. To make this representation unique, do not use decimal numbers that have all 9s after a certain position. For example, $0.49999 \ldots = 0.5$, and use only the latter form. Suppose there exists an ordering into a sequence of all these numbers. That this cannot be the case is shown by constructing a number that is between 0 and 1 but is not contained in the sequence. The number starts with zero. Its first digit after the decimal point is selected to be different from the first digit of the first number. Its second digit is selected to be different from the second digit of the second number, and so on. Its k-th digit is selected to be different from the k-th digit of the k-th number in the assumed sequence, for any value of k. The constructed number is not contained in the sequence because it is different from every number that is included in the sequence.

2. A more precise formulation follows later in the section.

3. The variables, before their average is taken, have to be standardized. That means subtracting their respective mean values and dividing by their respective standard deviations. The procedure of standardization in the case of normal variables will be discussed later.

4. A more precise value than 2 is 1.96. For practical purposes, the value of 2 may be used.

REFERENCES

BROWN, S. R., & MELAMED, L. (1990). *Experimental design and analysis* (Sage University Papers Series on Quantitative Applications in the Social Sciences, 07-074). Newbury Park, CA: Sage.

COOKE, R. M. (1991). *Experts in uncertainty: Opinion and subjective probability in science.* New York: Oxford University Press.

HENKEL, R. E. (1976). *Tests of significance* (Sage University Papers Series on Quantitative Applications in the Social Sciences, 07-004). Beverly Hills, CA: Sage.

JACOBY, W. G. (1997). *Statistical graphics for univariate and bivariate data.* (Sage University Papers Series on Quantitative Applications in the Social Sciences, 07-117). Thousand Oaks, CA: Sage.

KALTON, G. (1983). *Introduction to survey sampling* (Sage University Papers Series on Quantitative Applications in the Social Sciences, 07-035). Beverly Hills, CA: Sage.

KNOKE, D., & BURKE, P. J. (1980). *Log-linear models* (Sage University Papers Series on Quantitative Applications in the Social Sciences, 07-020). Beverly Hills, CA: Sage.

LAD, F. (1996). *Operational subjective statistical methods: A mathematical, philosophical, and historical introduction.* New York: Wiley.

LEVIN, I. P. (1999). *Relating statistics and experimental design: An introduction* (Sage University Papers Series on Quantitative Applications in the Social Sciences, 07-125). Thousand Oaks, CA: Sage.

LORD, F. M. (1968). *Statistical theories of mental test scores.* Reading, MA: Addison-Wesley.

ROSENBAUM, P. R. (1995). *Observational studies.* New York: Springer.

ABOUT THE AUTHOR

Tamás Rudas is Professor of Statistics and Dean of the Faculty of Social Sciences of the Eötvös Loránd University (ELTE) in Budapest, and is the Head of the Department of Statistics within the Faculty. He is also the Academic Director of TÁRKI Social Research Centre. His main research area is statistics and its applications in the social sciences, especially the analysis of categorical data. He has published in many theoretical, applied, and methodological journals, including the *Annals of Statistics, Journal of the Royal Statistical Society, Sociological Methodology, Communications in Statistics, Journal of Educational and Behavioral Statistics, and Quality and Quantity*. Dr. Rudas is also the author of *Odds Ratios in the Analysis of Contingency Tables* (Sage, 1998).